HOT TEA ACROSS INDIA

Rishad Saam Mehta graduated as an electronic engineer from Bombay University and is a travel writer and photographer. He lives in Mumbai and is especially fond of road trips, adventure sports, history and food, all of which tend to feature in his travel stories.

Hot Tea across India

RISHAD SAAM MEHTA

TRANQUEBAR

TRANQUEBAR PRESS
An imprint of westland ltd
Venkat Towers, 165, P.H. Road, Maduravoyal, Chennai 600 095
No. 38/10 (New No. 5), Raghava Nagar, New Timber Yard Layout, Bangalore 560 026
Survey No. A-9, II Floor, Moula Ali Industrial Area, Moula Ali, Hyderabad 500 040
23/181, Anand Nagar, Nehru Road, Santacruz East, Mumbai 400 055
4322/3, Ansari Road, Daryaganj, New Delhi 110 002

First published in India in TRANQUEBAR by westland ltd 2011

Illustrations by Gynelle Alves

Copyright © Rishad Saam Mehta 2011

10 9 8 7 6 5 4 3 2 1

ISBN: 978-93-81626-10-8

Typeset in Minion Regular by SÜRYA, New Delhi
Printed at Thomson Press (India) Ltd.

Contents

CONTENTS

*I*f there is one certainty about roads in India, it is that—no matter where you are or what the hour— if you want a cup of tea, you'll find a chai ka dukaan within a few kilometres. The tea shop is an integral part of Indian national highways, state highways, minor roads, even rough tracks. From the desolate unsealed roads of Spiti high up in the Himalayas, to the sinuous route to Munnar, a cup of tea is within easy reach.

When I travel, I like to drink tea, or rather, I need to drink tea; sometimes, I even survive just on tea. In fact, my travels in India are intricately linked with tea. A hot cup of well-brewed tea can truly be reviving in a way that a chilled aerated drink cannot. Even while driving through Rajasthan in the blazing desert summer, a khullad of chai in the shade of a tea tapri can refresh the mind and rejuvenate the body.

Hot tea has plenty of avatars across India. It can vary from a steaming hot cup of amber laced with fragrant spices like cardamom and ginger in Gujarat, to a glass of pale greenish liquid with yak's butter floating on top in a monastery in Ladakh. It can be served in a chipped white cup on a railway platform, a little clay pot (the khullad) across Rajasthan and Uttar Pradesh, or the standard 'cutting' glass which is the norm in Mumbai and south India. It might be strained by a delicate muslin cloth or flamboyantly poured from glass to glass to give it a fine froth. Tea shops can vary from fly-infested hovels to a hut surrounded by snow-capped mountains and with a river gurgling merrily behind it.

I don't think I can remember a single journey—and there have been many—where I haven't stopped for a cup of tea. This beverage that epitomises India and is appreciated from Kargil to Kanyakumari often breaks the monotony of long hours on the road and has often led to some very interesting moments. It has started delightful conversations and has also caused digestive consternation. Chai has recharged me in Kashmir and reassured me in Kerala. It has been brewed for me by a former bandit and a simple shepherd. It has chased away the demons in my head and made a frontier man my friend.

A cup of hot tea has been an integral part of every adventure I've had and every journey I've made in India.

The Highway Man and a Buffalo Instead of a Can

Tea stalls are the most lucrative of highway businesses. They will never go out of style and people sometimes run them as part of their retirement plans, as I found out on one of my first travel assignments.

The plan was to hitch a ride from Mumbai to Delhi in a truck and then write an article about the experience. I needed someone to go along with me for the jaunt. Now there are two people who immediately subscribe to my hare-brained travel ideas and at-the-drop-of-a-hat plans, no matter how outrageous or ridiculous they may sound, which is one of the reasons why they are my finest friends. One of them is Shapur, a former colleague, and the other is Chetan, born five days before me and infused with a never-ending enthusiasm to take a break from the mundane. I've known Chetan for twenty-three years, and he's never shied away from adventure, no matter how ridiculous or harebrained. From scaling a wall to get into a women's hostel when we were in college to jumping off a bridge into a raging river, he has been willing party to the plan.

So there we were, Chetan and I, one early morning, backpacks on our shoulders, trying to flag down trucks at Wadala in Mumbai. About a dozen completely ignored us; twenty or so passed by with the driver or cleaner enthusiastically waving back; one went past with the driver throwing a fistful of coins at us assuming we were homeless hobos. But perseverance paid off and finally, after about ninety minutes of us running through the entire gamut of attention-arresting actions, one truck stopped. The driver, Rathi Lal Khan, probably assumed we wanted to hitch a ride till the next junction, and was put completely on the backfoot when we settled down and declared that we'd be tagging along right till the capital. An offer to pay for all their meals during the trip and let them keep the bills secured us seats.

For three days we endured that small cabin, which

we shared with the truck driver and the cleaner, Sher Mohammed Akbar. Often, when the smell of diesel and sweat became overpowering, we would escape to the carrier on top of the cab with a bundle of the truckers' beedis. On starry nights, Sher Mohammed would join us on top of the cab with his flute and play haunting tunes that would scatter away into the night.

Sher Mohammed was a family man, and so his side of the truck had pictures of his wife and kids, as well as his parents. He was a gentleman, impeccably mannered and warm and courteous. Rathi Lal, on the other hand, was a randy rooster with a roving eye. His side of the cabin was populated with pictures of buxom ladies with bosoms and thighs so considerable that you'd need a land measuring tape to assess their girth. Every time we passed through a village or town, his eyes would lock onto any passing village belle like the guiding laser of a heat-seeking missile.

On the very first evening, when we stopped at Malegaon, Rathi Lal disappeared for an unusually long time. Finally the three of us went looking for him and found him in a country bar watching the energetic gyrations of the dancing girls within. Sher Mohammed seemed to command respect from Rathi Lal and also instil a little bit of fear in him. And, after a stern talking-to in a northern India dialect, Rathi Lal never disappeared again at any of our stops.

Behind the two front seats in the cabin, there was a flat bench where one of us could sleep. But, to be honest, that wasn't a resting place that called out to me, because above it hung a washing line. And lying on that bunk staring at truckers' underwear rendered threadbare by enthusiastic scrubbing at countless village wells wasn't exactly a sight to put one to sleep.

To avoid tax through Gujarat, the truckers had taken the route through Madhya Pradesh along the AB road, which is NH 3 or the Agra-Bombay road. We went past Nasik, Indore, Dewas, Biaora, Guna before getting to Gwalior, Dholpur and Agra. This was in 1998, and at that time most of NH 3's road surface resembled downtown Berlin at the end of the Second World War, and I think my bones were seriously rearranged during that journey thanks to the jars and thuds.

It was at 1 a.m. on the third night when we stopped for a cup of tea at a desolate place on the road between Gwalior and Agra, just a few kilometres short of Dholpur. We jumped out of the cabin and headed towards the solitary tea stall by the side of the road. Its dim, zero-watt bulb shone like a beacon beckoning weary travellers. There were a few patrons sitting on the charpois by the stall, all bundled in heavy shawls and with two common characteristics: all of them had magnificent moustaches and a barrel of a gun sticking out from under their shawls. Their various modes of transport were parked beside the tea stall: one battered old Mahindra Jeep, one Rajdoot motorcycle with colourful tassels on the handlebars and one handsome, healthy horse. It struck me then that we had stopped in the middle of the night in the heart of the Chambal valley, the notorious dacoit belt of India.

The owner of the tea stall had a moustache generously peppered with gray and a magnificent pot belly. A vertical smear of vermilion anointed his forehead. As his patrons drove, rode and galloped off, I saw him looking after them with a gaze that was filled with nostalgia. That, and the longing looks he kept casting at the rifle propped up in the corner of his tea stall, convinced me that this man who was now mixing together cups of tea to refresh weary travellers was probably once a highway man who had made a living out of looting them. Sher Mohammed concurred that this was probably the case, since dacoity wasn't as lucrative as it used to be, what with the increased security and a better armed police force in the region.

When the tea stall owner opened his little metal cash box to give me my change, he had to pick out coins from amongst mean-looking red live cartridges. I guessed that even though the man was now on the right side of the law, he still had more faith in his gun than the cops because this was a desolate and lonely stretch of road.

By way of friendly conversation, Chetan commented to the chaiwalla in an admiring way that he looked just like Kalia from the movie *Sholay*. The man just grunted, looked hard at us and then stared pointedly at his rifle. These loaded looks seemed to say, 'Son I've got a short temper and a long rifle.' I hurriedly gulped down my tea and we rapidly walked back to the truck.

The suspension of the truck, which had been battered by the pothole-riddled roads across Madhya Pradesh, finally gave up after a particularly bad stretch of road near Agra, and we spent a whole day at a roadside mechanics shop while it was getting repaired. Chetan and I could have taken a taxi to Delhi, but with our three-digit budgets, time was expendable, money was not.

I still think of that truck quite fondly. It was an old Tata 1613 that had passed its prime a long time ago, but was carrying on resiliently. Many of its surfaces wore wielding marks like battle scars. At places where the exteriors were scratched, I could see that it had been painted many times over. When we stopped at truckers' dhabas and parked the truck amongst other newer, flashier trucks, our 1613 always stood out like a rotten tooth in an otherwise perfect smile.

But the old girl still had spirit. There were times when Rathi Lal would pull out and overtake two trucks in a row, the speedo wavering at 90kmph. It handled steep inclines without baulking and on the occasional rare smooth stretch, its exhaust had an almost musical purr to it as it cruised along. In fact, sleeping on top of the cab on a balmy night, it would practically have a lullaby-like effect.

But at every pothole we hit, the truck would creak and groan. Honestly, I was quite surprised that we'd almost made it to Agra before some part of the truck gave way.

Hence, we crossed over from Uttar Pradesh into Haryana about an hour before sunrise the next day. This was also the last border control, and as Rathi Lal and Sher Mohammed lugged the bulky file that contained papers, permits, PUC certificates, licenses and logs to show the officials and most definitely bribe them to get the necessary clearances, I went to look for a cup of morning tea. Chetan was still asleep, so I didn't wake him up.

That cup of tea led to the most embarrassing travel moment I have had to date.

The tea stall was a simple bamboo hut with a thatched

roof affair. The chaiwalla was boiling tea leaves in a sturdy copper vessel on a high-pressure stove. I asked for a cup of tea, and he told me that the milk for the day was on its way. I expected a banyan and dhoti-clad milkman, wearing shoes but no socks, to arrive on a cycle and deliver milk from a large aluminium can. This was a rural area after all, I knew better than to expect plastic bags of milk.

The dudhwalla did come, and he was dressed to my expectations right down to his shoes. But instead of an aluminium can, he had with him a big, black, hairy buffalo. The tea stall's supply of milk literally came straight from the source.

The tea was very refreshing, but the full-fat, unprocessed milk did not sit well and within minutes it translated into my stomach giving out pops, bangs and squeaks like the old truck's battered suspension. With the pressure building up inside, I knew it would just be a matter of time before I'd lose the battle of the clench.

So I set off to find a secluded spot to go and do my business like I had done during the past few days on the road. I had learnt important lessons about behind-the-bushes-bathrooms, and one of them was to never 'go' on a grassy field that is soggy. After a while, your feet start to sink and you really aren't in a position to move.

It was still quite dark, and I walked down the road and found myself a hard piece of ground a few meters off the road. I sat down to what was going to be my last spur-of-the-moment toilet. Half-way through my endeavour, a light suddenly came on and as my eyes adjusted to the scene around me, I realised I had chosen the front porch of a roadside dhaba as my impromptu voiding ground. I had been blissfully gaining relief bang in the centre of a semi-circle formed by charpois on which slept the cook, the cashier and the waiters of the aforementioned dhaba. The person who had switched on the light was staring at me, mouth open in horror, probably trying to work out whether this was a part of his nightmare or if I was for real.

'What are you doing?' he asked me in a horrified whisper.

I tried to coo out a soothing sentence in a lilting voice that would hopefully have a lullaby effect and put the appalled man back to sleep. It only served for him to sit up in his charpoi, rubbing his eyes in disbelief, convinced that this scene comprising of me, my bottle and my pants bunched around my knees was malodorous reality.

I knew I had about forty seconds before the man's brain started firing on all cylinders and he was wide awake. I rapidly grabbed my bottle and splashed through the final act of my 'job'. By now the other shapes huddled under thick layers of blankets had started to stir, and I had a sudden vision of being surrounded with my pants down by angry men who weren't very amused to have woken up to the glorious sight of me and my water bottle. I stood up just as the man whose day I had started with such a gloriously revealing sight was reaching for his lathi and shouting to wake up the others. I ran towards where the trucks were parked. In my mental state, I couldn't tell which one was ours; all of them looked similar. In hot pursuit behind me were the man and three others.

I sent out a loud, piercing whistle, and in a few seconds I saw Chetan climb on top of my truck's cab in answer to my whistle. He took in the whole scene in a flash and realised that we needed a quick getaway. Fortunately Rathi Lal and Sher Mohammed were back; Chetan told them to fire up the truck's engine and pull out of the parking space immediately. As I ran up alongside Sher Mohammed, Chetan grabbed my hands and hoisted me clear through the door of the cab. In a desperate attempt to stop me, the man threw his lathi which hit the side of the truck but missed me. The truck picked up speed and we got clear away.

Since then, I have always double-checked the source of the milk at any roadside tea stall I've stopped at.

Chef Doltu of Chandra Tal

I met Shapur when I started to work with the magazine *Autocar India* in 2001. Since then he and I have become fast friends. All I have to do is mention the Himalayas or the possibility of sighting wildlife and he's on a plane to the closest airport to join me for a driving trip. The foundation of this has been a common unshakable fondness for food—weight and waistline notwithstanding—and an interest in Second World War history and aircraft and automobiles.

In the August of 2005, I set off from Delhi for a driving trip across what—in my opinion—is the most spectacular road in India. The road that runs from Gramphu to Kaza through the districts of Lahaul and Spiti in Himachal Pradesh. I had called Shapur, and he'd immediately decided he wanted to come along. He got on a flight to Chandigarh from where I picked him up. We'd then driven the 320 kilometres to Manali over nine hours—a pile up through the narrow lanes of Kullu had cost us an extra three hours—spent the night there, and then started towards Spiti early the next morning.

Gramphu—fifteen kilometres after the Rohtang Pass while heading from Manali to Keylong—is more a collection of tea shops than a village. If you turn right here, you're on the road to Kaza. It is this road that often makes me believe that if there were a god of landscaping amongst the multitude of gods that make up the Hindu pantheon, then the Himalayan district of Spiti would quite simply be the pinnacle of his or her art.

It is a road that runs past glacial plains and along frothy rivers and through sudden patches of green grasslands. It crosses vast valleys and snakes up imposing ranges. Whenever I am on that road, I feel small and inconsequential. It reminds me that, in the grand scale of things, my life on this planet is but a blink of an eye. It makes me want to live my life to the fullest. It makes me want to write so evocatively about its charms, and capture the vistas in such stunning photographs, that people who read my stories will be tempted to visit this region and experience for themselves one of the most stunning locales in India.

The tarmac ends two kilometres after the right turn off the Manali-Leh road, and from then on the road is unsealed. Little settlements en route are Chattru, Chotta Dara and Batal. Incidentally, the solitary dhaba at Chotta Dara—run by a local shepherd family—serves strong and spicy masala chai. Or maybe it's the splendid location of that little dhaba that enhances the taste of the tea. It beckons the weary traveller with a happy gaggle of multicoloured prayer flags flapping in the breeze. The best place to sit is on the little terrace outside the dhaba, where you can see mountains all round, soaring up to the heavens and capped with ice that has known no other state of being like snow or water. And you can still see the paths that gigantic glaciers—as big as skyscrapers—took when they gouged out valleys during the last Ice Age.

The inside of the dhaba smells of spice and sheep. There are thick mattresses placed on low wooden ledges along the wall where travellers can spend the night for a nominal amount. Heavy quilts are provided to keep you warm; quilts so weighty with the mass of cotton needed to insulate you from the bitter cold, that you really can't toss and turn under them.

Three kilometres after Batal, just before the mighty

Kunzum La, the solitary pass on this road standing tall at 14,931 feet, is a little offshoot from Chandra Tal, the moon lake which sits tranquil and blue, nestled like a robin's egg amidst high mountains. The lake itself is at 14,107 feet, and to camp here you need to carry all your provisions with you. There is no friendly tea shop here; there isn't a single permanent structure, and I hope it remains like that. Chandra Tal is as close to heaven as you can get while yet in a mortal form.

Since we needed to set up camp here, we had hired the services of Doltu, a local Himachali lad. He'd met up with us in Manali, and loaded his pots, pans, primus stove, his tent and other camp-kitchen paraphernalia in the cavernous rear of my Toyota Innova. He had then looked us over intently with his chin clasped between his thumb and forefinger and set off to buy provisions. He had been making an estimate of how much he'd have to buy for two days of camping judging by our size.

Luckily it was a weekday and the road to Rohtang was devoid of all traffic except some trucks that were crawling towards the pass. We carried on for five kilometres past Gramphu to get to Koksar—a slight detour—since Koksar was where we could buy choice cuts of fresh mutton from Bhadur Singh Thakur's Zhatka Meat Shop. After that we drove back to Gramphu and took the road towards Spiti.

The thirteen-kilometre 'road' to Chandra Tal, just before the Kunzum La, is actually a walking track that has been marginally widened to accommodate vehicles. Many would consider it downright ridiculous to call it a road—we had to proceed with utmost caution because the track was just about wide enough to accommodate the breadth of the Toyota, and we really didn't want to get too close to the crumbly edges. The Border Roads Organisation (BRO) has hacked out these roads from sheer mountain sides which have relented very reluctantly. The drops are vertigo-inducing and so deep that a pebble thrown down takes about ten seconds to come to a complete rest. These are steep inclines, but the strong engine of the car took them in its stride, and torque, even at this high altitude, was never a problem.

We were now driving at over 13,000 feet above mean sea level, and I knew from past experience that soon we'd meet the demon that lives at this altitude. It can't be seen or heard, but attacks in the form of headaches, nausea, restlessness and breathlessness—Altitude Mountain Sickness (AMS). Tablets like Disprin and Diamox only suppress symptoms; the best way to win the battle against AMS is to ascend allowing ample time for acclimatisation. Unfortunately, despite knowing this, we'd had to ascend pretty quickly because Shapur had limited leave, so this trip featured many long hours at the wheel, rapid ascends and night-long drives. We'd taken our doses of Disprin and Diamox, but I knew from past experience that any sort of exertion and the demon would batter down the defences set up by these pills.

About seven hours after we'd left Manali, we reached Chandra Tal and chose a little grassy patch on the western shore of the lake to pitch tents. Thank god for Doltu, the man was an expert at setting up camp; if it had been left to us two urbanites, we'd have sent the tent flapping away merrily in the strong wind that had started up.

By the time we'd set up camp—which required us making two trips to the car-parking place and back—the exertion helped AMS batter down all defences and I was completely in its deadly grip. AMS is quite the whimsical monster. You might not feel it on your first five trips, and then suddenly, on the sixth, it might decide to grasp you in its clutches. So, at Chandra Tal, Shapur escaped with just a minor headache, but I faced its full wrath. It was like a punishment for not respecting the height and ascending too fast. My stomach retched, my head pounded as if there were a jungle drum being played inside, and the mountains around seemed to spin like a carousel. Doltu was least affected since he was the most acclimatised. Undaunted, he primed his stove and prepared piping hot tomato soup. Amongst his provisions, he'd bought a packet of cream and decoratively laced the soup with it. Every spoonful of the soup seemed to wash away my headache and refresh my mind. The sun had already dipped behind the tall mountains by then, and the cold had started creeping in. The silence was only broken by the steady drone of the stove, and the aroma of spicy mutton curry and rice laced with saffron and pure desi ghee floating towards us on wafts of wind hinted that the dinner that Doltu was diligently preparing for us would be ready soon.

By the time it was dark, we were roundly cursing Mr H. Singh, a certain tall, hairy and loud gentleman from Chandigarh, who had advised us on the route and had convinced us that, since it was summer, the temperature would be very pleasant. 'Oye, summer hain yaar! What jacket-shacket, gloves-shoves. All you'll need are T-shirts and shorts.' I was now pleasantly freezing my ears off as the temperature dipped to seven degrees. During the course of the night, it would go down to two degrees. Lesson learnt was that summer is frivolous at Chandra Tal. It lasts as long as the sun is shining merrily in the blue sky. Once the sun bids adieu, the cold creeps in.

In the morning, when I woke up, I was so frozen that I didn't do my routine stretching out of fear that pieces of me would crack and fall off.

The steady hum of the stove told us that Doltu was

already at work. He cheerily yelled out, 'Good morning, Sir,' as he walked over bearing steaming cups on a tray. Even before he'd thrown back the flap of our tent and handed Shapur the tray, I knew that he'd also brought along a packet of Everest Tea Masala from the aroma that preceded him. That morning cup of sweet masala chai that he served might have been made out of milk powder and tea bags, but it was so well brewed, it refreshed my mind and cleared the drowsiness and heavy-headedness. When I exited the tent, the lake and the blue skies around seemed even prettier. Though it was daylight, the sun was yet to climb over the mountains. The lake was absolutely still, and the blue sky, the towering mountains and the scattered clouds were reflected perfectly in its glass-like surface. It seemed as if an identical world existed within the depths of the Chandra Tal.

We spent that morning exploring the little trails around Chandra Tal or lounging by the lake. There is a trek that starts at Chandra Tal and ends at Baralacha La, the second pass on the Manali-Leh route at 16,040 feet. This is a three-day trek over thirty-two kilometres, and the last section has streams that need to be forded with the help of ropes. In the afternoon, three groups of dishevelled trekkers arrived at Chandra Tal. They'd done the trek in the opposite direction. While the trekkers were absolutely drained and disappeared into their tents not to come out till the next morning, the guides and the porters were in fine fettle. That night we sat at the campfire that they'd lit, sipping on a drink that consisted of one part Old Monk rum and three parts Chandra Tal water.

They talked about treks they'd been on, ghosts that they'd seen, and every now and then burst into song. These started out as very melodious and lilting, as if their voices had been trained in song, but as the level of the rum bottle dipped steadily, all melody escaped into the wild.

The next morning, once we'd broken camp, we dropped Doltu at the little dhaba just before the girder bridge at Batal. He would catch the Kaza-Manali bus and head back to Manali. We were going to spend four more days in Spiti, driving right till Kaza, the district headquarters. When we finally drove back to Manali, we arrived there in the early afternoon of the fifth day and called Doltu who came to collect his equipment from the car. Shapur and I thanked him profusely because it was due to his outdoor and culinary skills that those two days at Chandra Tal remain my best days out camping ever.

Thoda Chai Paani

We started the 600-kilometre drive from Manali to Delhi in the late evening. Our logic was that we'd arrive on the outskirts of Delhi by the dawn of the next day and get to our office guesthouse in south Delhi before rush hour began. This would allow a few hours of shut-eye before catching the afternoon flight to Mumbai.

By the time we'd stopped for dinner at Swarghat, the last major town in Himachal Pradesh, it was quite late into the night, and at the check-post border between Himachal Pradesh and Punjab, a portly policeman flagged us down. He shone his torch into the car and then on our faces. He then demanded to see my driver's licence, since I was at the wheel.

When Kanwaljit Singh checked my licence, the money meter probably started ticking in his brain. My licence was from Mumbai, the car with a KA 42 number plate was registered in Ramnagaram, Karnataka, and we were two unshaven and bedraggled youths crossing over from Himachal Pradesh to Punjab at 2.45 in the morning. Besides this, the tent and our sleeping bags dumped behind had opened out, giving the car the appearance of a stake-out and getaway vehicle. He was sure that some fine or, at the very least, a baksheesh could be extorted from us. He looked at the registration and car documents for a full twenty minutes. Then, he asked for Shapur's licence. That was given. Slightly disgruntled now, he asked again to see my licence.

Everything was in order.

Then a brainwave seemed to strike him. He gravely declared that photocopies of the car documents were not acceptable. To which I promptly responded by pulling the originals out of my bag. Not one to give up, he finally pulled his trump card.

'PUC certificate kidhar hain? Hazaar rupiye ka fine lag jayega!'

But I knew I had seen a recent PUC (pollution under control) certificate, and I started looking for it. Kanwaljit

Singh began to look smug, even giving out hearty chortles of happiness in anticipation of the money he was going to make. 'Oye come on, come on, let it be. You don't have the PUC certificate, just hand me the fine and we can both go our separate ways,' he said.

'Just give me five minutes, Sir. I know I have it,' I replied politely and started looking under the rubber matting of the car.

The chortles faded away and were replaced by snorts of surprise.

Shapur got out, opened the bonnet of the Innova, and with the light of his cell phone, started peering around in the engine bay.

'What is he doing?' demanded the policeman, his face such a picture of bewildered astonishment that his eyebrows had practically disappeared into his turban.

'Sir,' I replied, my expression grave and serious, 'pollution comes from the exhaust gases which are a by-product of internal combustion which happens inside the engine over here. Right?'

'Yes,' Kanwaljit Singh replied, his face now showing the strain that his brain was going through. It wore an expression that hovered between incredulity and mild panic and he glanced up at the full moon above for a long moment and then back at my face wondering if I had been touched by a spot of lunar lunacy.

'So,' I continued, in a tone that one uses when

talking to someone who has less active brain cells than the number of wheels on a car, 'he is looking for the certificate in the engine.'

'Just give me the fine and get going, otherwise I will lock you up in the kothi!' Kanwaljit Singh shouted, spittle flying out of his mouth and his face going red, signalling that he was reaching the end of his tether.

'Just two minutes more, Sir, please,' I said, in a voice now dripping with respect since the jail angle had been introduced. I pulled out a rubber mat, put it on the road under the car and then slid under the Innova to examine the under-body in case the PUC certificate was hidden there.

By now Kanwaljit Singh was tapping his gun holster very suggestively. Finally, Shapur and I got into the car and I pulled out my wallet, wincing at the fact that Kanwaljit Singh hadn't tired of all this tomfoolery and told us to get going, as we'd hoped. He was determined to extract some sort of fine from us. It seemed that I would have to give in to the policeman's demand. I opened my wallet —and found the PUC certificate. I remembered now, putting it there for safe-keeping. Triumphantly I handed it to him. Kanwaljit Singh, as dejected as a puppy whose bone has been rudely snatched away, checked it minutely and, finding it in order, decided to stop beating around the bush.

'Okay, theek hai. Thoda chai paani kar do.'

Shapur replied without missing a beat. In a heartfelt voice laced with gratitude he said, 'Thank you Police Uncleji, very kind of you, but hamne abhi abhi khana khaya hain. Next time hum ayega toh chai aur paani ke saath biscuit bhi lega. Please Good Day biscuit le ke aana, woh butter aur kaaju waala. But abhi stomach full hain, so no thank you.'

He had deftly turned around the policeman's demand for baksheesh into an invitation for us to have tea with *him*. Kanwaljit Singh's jaw would have dropped to the ground in surprise had it not come to rest on his belly. I could almost hear the wheels of his mind whirring as he tried to make sense of what he had heard. He was so stunned that I had to pluck the PUC certificate out of his hands. He just stood there, mouth working but the words refusing to emerge.

I was laughing so hard that the car stalled twice before I could start off. The last vision I had of Kanwaljit Singh was in my rear view mirror as we drove away. He was scratching his beard, probably wondering what dinner, Good Day biscuit and cashews had to do with his demand for some baksheesh.

Spirituality and Splashes

Chetan and I have a common friend, Mouneet Mehta, who is a whiz at computers, and really can't decide whether the adventure bug has bitten him or not. As in, he has the initial enthusiasm to do something thrilling and exciting, but it suddenly deserts him, like a skydiver's parachute that has refused to open, leaving him anxious and panicky.

In October 2008, the three of us travelled together eleven years after our first trip together, which was a trek to Dodi Tal from Uttarkashi and then a bus ride to Manali.

Mouneet, Chetan and two other friends were spending a few days at a resort in Devprayag, which is a holy town on the confluence of the Alaknanda and Bhagirathi rivers which merge to form the Ganga and flow on towards Rishikesh and Haridwar. I was in the Garhwal on a work assignment, so we decided to meet up at Rishikesh, or rather Camp Silver Sands, which is twenty-seven kilometres from Rishikesh towards Devprayag. This tented rafting camp is run by an old friend of mine, Vaibhav Kala, and is located on a beach by the river Ganga.

Over the last eight years, Silver Sands has become a base for me whenever I am in the Garhwal Himalayas. I know that I can turn up there at any odd hour and find a comfortable bed and a hot meal. Arriving at the camp itself is a minor adrenaline rush. After parking the car on the road above, you walk down through the forested hillside towards the beach where the camp is set up. On the higher reaches of the river bank are the kitchen and staff tents, and the former always sends out the delicious aroma of pakoras frying or strong tea being brewed.

Lower down, set in a neat single file along the length of the bank, are the guest tents. The mess tent stands close to the water's edge and this is where one can hang out, reading, sipping tea or just listening to the gurgle of the river as it tumbles over the rocks and pebbles beyond the beach. It's the perfect place to relax, and we figured it would be a nice two-day break: we could take it easy by the river and do a spot of river rafting as well. All of us were quite keen on the rafting, except Mouneet, who hasn't yet gotten round to learning how to swim. To subject himself to all that water without knowing how to stay afloat was, in his mind, like a death wish.

But that was before we sat down for a barbeque on the beach that first evening at camp. The barbeque area was set up next to the mess tent, with chairs arranged in a circle around a bonfire, and it is here that Mouneet set course towards being convinced to give river rafting a go.

I have often noticed that the stiffer the drink in the hand, the more the bravado. I've been in umpteen situations where I've heard people loudly declare that they are fed up with their routine and mundane existence and all I have to do is make the call and they'd be ready for a road trip at the drop of a hat. 'What's the point of existing without excitement? I'm ready to kick routine, hit the road and live on the wild side', are some of the things I've heard, and my answer is always a condescending smile. Because when I do actually make the call, I rarely find the spontaneity that seemed to overflow at the party with the drink in hand. There is usually a 'horrible, demanding boss' not granting leave or a 'sulking spouse' throwing a tantrum.

Back to the beach camp by the Ganga. Mouneet was also going through that momentary bravado, helped along with his friends' slurred sentences like, 'Do it man', 'You live only once', 'Think of the stories you can tell the ladies', 'It's the river Ganga and she'll protect a God-fearing soul like you'.

All this finally convinced Mouneet that river rafting was a piece of cake and the next morning he found himself on a bright blue raft with a paddle in hand listening to the river guide, Kana Singh, shout out commands like, 'Easy forward', 'Right back' and 'Get down'.

His face was a picture of profound piety, and it had very little to do with the Ganga's mythological connection to the heavens above. He was feverishly praying for deliverance because the gurgling roar was getting louder by the second as the raft sped towards the 'Wall'.

The meanest and most irrational rapid amongst the many rapids on the Ganga as she twists and tumbles her way down from Devprayag to Rishikesh, the Wall is both revered and feared. Guides usually try to read it from the road above before the start of the day's rafting, because there is no standard procedure or path through the Wall. Its intensity and the pattern of the currents change every day, sometimes several times within the day—now even more so thanks to the fluctuations caused by the Tehri Dam. The Wall earned its name from the fact that going past it is like trying to go through a wall of water. Five times out of ten, rafts flip while attempting this rapid.

As the raft sped towards the Wall, Mouneet's soul was calling out to all the gods and goddesses in the Hindu pantheon to deliver him from this icy cold frothing mess that he had allowed himself to be foolishly led into. By then the noise created by the liquid confusion of the Grade 4+ rapid was so loud that even Kana Singh had to call out his commands at the top of his voice. Mouneet's pleading piety precipitated into pure panic as realisation dawned that this little rubber raft, which was essentially a buttressed carpet of air, wasn't going to be able to handle the million cubits of churning chaos that it was about to be hurled into. Chetan and I were the first row of paddlers: he on the right and I on the left. Mouneet was part of the second row and was sitting behind me. I glanced back and saw his eyes widen with apprehension. I looked ahead. The Wall loomed large. The waves were seven foot and more, and there were huge holes being created as the river leapt high in the air and then crashed back down on itself.

Mouneet tightened the grip on his paddle to prepare himself for battle as the raft—now in the clutch of the currents—was suddenly pulled towards the rapid. It rode the first seven-foot swell gallantly, but it all started to go awry at the second wave. A ten-foot sheet of water had the raft vertical, but Chetan and I managed to heave our shoulders forward and, with a little help from momentum, it began to fall back the right way. But, before it could, a huge renegade wave came charging in diagonally and flicked the raft over as casually as you would flick a bug off your forearm. Mouneet's eyes went even wider as he saw me three feet in the air above him. He tried to grab the guy lines of the raft but he couldn't find them and a moment later went face first into the cold green waters of the Ganga.

In the first moment of pure terror, Mouneet must have swallowed enough water to fill a bathtub. I knew that panic must be gripping him like a python coiling around his chest, and as I bobbed to the surface I tried looking for him. The raft was upside down and Chetan emerged from under it. I was still in the rapid and the waves were breaking over me, but thankfully all of us were on the other side of the Wall.

In the safety briefing, Kana Singh had reassured us that the life jacket would prevent any paddler from drowning, and as if in accordance with that thought, Mouneet broke the surface of the water, frantically waving his arms and taking in deep gulps of air. Villagers on the cliffs by the river had seen the raft go over and mistook his panic-stricken gestures for signs of friendliness and enthusiastically waved back. To this Mouneet replied with some choice phrases which I am going to pretend I did not hear. Finally he calmed down, reassured that he was in the river rather than looking down at it from the heavens above. I saw him go into the whitewater position, which essentially is to lie on your back and let the current carry you out of the rapid till you're rescued.

Relieved that he was fine, I took in the scene around me. The raft was still upside down and Kana Singh was trying to turn it the right way up. The two safety kayakers were making sure that all of us were alright. Two rafts who were behind us took on the Wall as well: one made it and the other was flipped over. Now there were two rafts floating upside down in the water and twelve of us floating downstream. Safety kayakers helped the more tired swimmers with a tow and got everyone into their respective rafts.

Back in the safety of the raft, Mouneet launched into a series of loud belches, releasing the air that he had swallowed along with water. They echoed up and down the river valley like the heartfelt mating calls of a lonesome leopard.

After twenty minutes and two more rapids, which now seemed like the mild ripples of a calm sea, we pulled up in front of our camp. Mouneet glanced at the rocks in the river, trying to spot a waterline because he was sure that with the amount of water he had swallowed, the river's level must have dropped. He also had some colourful unquotable quotes for us who'd cajoled him into this adventure.

But as we sat under the mess tent by the river, sipping the hot tea that the staff had kept ready for us, his mind had already started giving heroic shape to his inelegant dunking in the river. For months after that he milked the incident for all its worth. The last time I heard him recount it, the incident featured his being chased by crocodiles that had attacked the raft and flipped it over.

Bussing it to Manali

More than a decade before the trip to Rishikesh, Chetan, Mouneet and I did a trek together from Uttarkashi to Dodi Tal and Yamnotri. After the trek, we decided to spend a few days in Manali. All three of us were students then, and Manali had that aura of being the epicentre of 'cool'. We just *had* to hang out in Manali, we felt, and cross it off our list of places to visit.

This trip was four years before going on driving holidays became my job with *Autocar India*. At the time I didn't have a car, and money was always a scarce commodity for us, so we couldn't even consider taking a private taxi from Haridwar (where our trek ended) to Manali.

The Himachal Pradesh Transport Office in Haridwar proudly stated that it had one 'LUXAREY' bus a day to Manali. The word brought to mind images of a sleek, comfortable bus with two rows of headlights, an array of turning lights and 'Pinky' or 'Sweety' artistically written in orange reflector tape on the rear windshield. Of course, the inside would be carpeted and fitted with aeroplane-type seats, and if we were really lucky, maybe the onboard entertainment programme would include an Amitabh Bachchan movie. After all, the board above the booking office did state 'LUXAREY' in bold Times New Roman.

There was a mad rush at the ticket counter, since queuing can be a foreign concept in many parts of India. So I had to pull, push and elbow myself to the ticket window after which I obtained three tickets for what we hoped would be a relaxing trip. On politely enquiring where the bus was parked, we were told that if we went around to the back of the booking office we would see it. So off we went in search of the bus, arguing about whether to keep our sweaters with us or to pack them up; it would get pretty cold in the air-conditioning, we thought.

A lesson we learned that day was that the Himachal

Pradesh Travel Corporation obviously uses the word 'luxury' very broadly. Our bus was actually one that had been salvaged from the wrecker's yard; its two headlights gave out less luminance than a bunch of fireflies. The indicators were manual levers that had arrows painted on them. The seats inside were of solid wood, and any cushioning you got was directly proportional to the prosperity of your backside. In that respect, all three of us were paupers.

Most of the other passengers were simple hill folk for whom the bus really was a luxury—because for them anything that moved on its own accord without the help of a four-legged creature was a luxury. The bus was officially a two by three, meaning it had a row of two seats on the left and three on the right. However, the booking office kept selling tickets right till the driver fired up the engine and tooted the horn indicating that the bus was about to leave, so obviously there were more passengers than seats.

On the seats next to us was a pair of sanyasis, junior and senior. I call them sanyasis because they were dressed in saffron clothes and their heads were clean-shaven with a bull's-eye of hair in the centre. They were carrying a lot of pots of what appeared to be Ganga jal. Every time the driver hit a pothole or a speed-breaker, there was a flood in the bus. By the time we reached Manali, seventeen-and-a-half hours later, each and every person on that bus had been cleansed of his or her sins because all our feet were soaked in the water.

After we'd stopped for dinner and the hours got long, passengers started dropping off to sleep. I found it difficult, thanks to the cramped seating position, so I amused myself watching other people sleep. It made entertaining viewing to see people contort themselves into all types of positions in an attempt to get comfortable on the hard wooden seats. On the third row behind us were four youths and they were so entwined that it took me an hour to figure out which limb belonged to whom. Mouneet and I amused ourselves by aiming pistachio shells at the bull's-eye on junior's head or senior's open mouth, five and ten points respectively. Luckily, both were fast asleep, junior with a smile on his face—heavenly dreams about apsaras, maybe!

The driver was evidently an ill-tempered chap; he literally aimed the bus at every pothole in the road and floored the gas pedal over speed-breakers. He also seemed to be minuscule of bladder, so he would often pull off the road to relieve himself with some of the passengers following suit. Most times, these stops were at places where there were dhabas or solitary tea stalls. Mouneet and I would get down at every tea stall to get a hot cup of tea. It is on that trip that I grew fond of these solitary Himalayan tea stalls that stand as a source of solace in the middle of nowhere. It's a mild thrill to stand there, shrouded by chilly darkness, enjoying a warm cup of brew. Everything is dark and unknown beyond the small circle of light thrown by a kerosene lamp or dim bulb. We would huddle around the wood stove for warmth along with other passengers and patrons shrouded in shawls. The only sounds disturbing the silence of the night would be the hum of the hand-operated bellows of the stove and the soft slurping of hot tea.

When we got to Kullu, which is about forty kilometres from Manali, most of the passengers got down and I thought that we would, at last, have a comfortable ride. Wrong again; you see, our bus had a split personality. While it was in Haryana and Punjab, it was an interstate superfast bus, so there were limited stops. But when it entered the Kullu district, it became a local bus. Anyone on the road could put out his or her hand and it would stop to pick the person up. Soon it was filled with screaming school children and other locals, and almost more jam-packed than it had been when we'd started out from Haridwar.

The last straw was when a shepherd climbed in with eight goats. The flooding started again, but it wasn't pure Ganga jal this time—it was the goats copiously venting themselves and bleating in satisfaction while at it. A Billy goat wandered between my legs and started showing an unhealthy interest in my belt with its horns pointing at a very awkward place. The stench that Billy was radiating cleared my sinuses like a blowtorch melting butter and made my eyes water. Mouneet, who had a goat across his knees, was clutching his monkey cap to his nose, and Chetan, sharing the seat with the shepherd whose stench made the goats' odour smell like a rose garden in comparison, was slowly turning a pretty shade of green.

I really couldn't bear it any more. I had survived the night on countless cups of tea and cigarettes every time the bus had stopped but now my behind was sore from the hard seats, I felt like I'd smelt every odour that the human race was capable of permeating. And now a Billy goat was parked between my legs, bleating away to glory. When the bus stopped next I got off and rode the remaining journey on the roof. Lying amidst soft gunny bags filled with woollen wear that Tibetans were taking to sell in the markets of Manali, and taking in the fine views all around, that was beyond doubt the best part of my bus trip in the Himalayas.

Battle of the Loaders and Scrupulous Railway Clerks

I have long come to terms with the fact that one day there will be a bed waiting for me at Dr Dixit's Dwelling for the Demented. But till I'm actually forced to check in, I'm going to happily keep on doing stuff that makes people point their index finger to their temple and twirl it around rapidly.

I realised this while crossing an icy-cold mountain stream that had overflowed onto the road just after Keylong on the Manali-Leh road. Of course, my electric blue Royal Enfield Bullet scoffed at such minor problems. I had bought it in Pune in 1998 because it was the only motorcycle in India that could face up to an arduous journey like this. But halfway through the stream, I realised you probably need to be a little crazy to enjoy sojourns like these.

The high road to Leh that goes over five mountain passes is the epitome of motorcycling in India. You may have ripped down the Delhi-Jaipur road, perhaps you've scraped pedals around corners on the twisty road to Ooty via Masinagudi, and possibly you've even dodged elephants on the road to Kaziranga in Assam, but you haven't done the mother of all Indian two-wheeler rides if you haven't ridden a Bullet to Leh.

I've biked in the Himalayas before and, this trip, I decided to send my motorcycle from Mumbai to Delhi by train and start my ride from Delhi. On my last biking trip, I had ridden my Bullet back to Mumbai from Delhi and it had been quite a monotonous ride. I hadn't anticipated, though, that getting the bike on the train at Mumbai and off at Delhi would turn out to be *such* an adventure.

Like most Indians, I'm used to the request for 'chai-paani'—i.e., a tip—from people rendering any small service. Mishra, the baniyan and pyjama-clad railway loader that I met at the Bandra-Kurla terminus, was no exception.

Mishra had approached me soon after I had wheeled my Enfield Bullet into the station. A bespectacled clerk at the booking office had taken my money for the freight charges with his right hand and simultaneously gestured impossibility with the left. The freight bogeys for the Paschim Express were full, he explained; there was a huge freight surplus which had to be processed and sent first. 'Pack your gaadi and leave it next to the luggage officers' cabin; we'll dispatch it within a week. Next please ...'

My face must have reflected the horror of having all my plans go awry. I was flying to Delhi the next morning and had planned to ride from Delhi to Leh and then to Kashmir; I had a schedule to keep, pictures to take and paradise to explore. And here, at step one, in the environs of one of the largest rail networks of the world, it was already all coming undone.

Just then, a man sidled up to me. The first thing that struck me about him was his hair: hormones had made a serious navigational error, because while his pate was shiny and bald, his shoulders were a barber's playground. With the confidence of an expert black marketer outside a multiplex, the man, Mishra, told me that he could get my bike onto the train for a fee of seven hundred rupees. I agreed without hesitation— I knew I'd have to recruit someone like him if I had any hope of my bike being loaded into the train due to leave for Amritsar in two hours—and that was my mistake. Though he managed to hide it well, I caught the grimace of regret that flashed on his face for not having demanded more. His recovery was brilliant, though. 'Of course I'll need some more for chai-paani since you'll be very happy that your bike has been loaded,' he quickly added. This man was demanding a tip even before he had rendered his services!

Rather than have some illusionary amount hanging in the air that may later create a sticky situation, I asked him how much he wanted for 'chai-paani'. His answer was a shocking one thousand rupees. I asked him if he wanted a cup of tea, or if he wanted me to help finance the opening of a chain of tea houses. And so the verbal jousting began and we finally shook hands at Rs 1100 for the entire deal.

Though he told me to relax and go home, I couldn't leave until I was sure that my bike was on the train. So I watched while Mishra's men packed the motorcycle expertly, stuffing straw as a buffer for the more delicate parts like the headlight and the turn signal stalks.

The pile of luggage that had to be loaded into the Paschim kept growing at a rapid rate and by the time the train pulled onto the platform, I knew there was no way that all that mass would fit into what seemed like a match-box sized luggage bogey of the train.

Now there were two gangs of loaders, and the leaders

of each—one the bald Mishra, and the other the bearded Bheema—were the two powers on the platform. These two had about twenty loaders each working under them. Though they all sat and shared food, played cards and got drunk together, when there was a train to be loaded, the platform became their battleground. Expletives flew across like shrapnel while cargo parcels were hurled like cannonballs at the doorway of the bogey, where the friendly team would try and catch them while at the same time trying to deflect the enemy's cargo.

Amidst this pandemonium of high-velocity flying cargo, Mishra had recruited seven of his top chargers to rush at the open doorway with my 175kg Bullet and storm the bogey. Three on each side and one behind, they rushed in at an angle while the other men intensified the normal cargo-loading to distract Bheema's boys. As they reached the doorway, two of their team swiftly reached down and lifted the front wheel off the platform into the higher level of the bogey and just as the rival gang of loaders noticed the entry of this huge parcel, the bike was inside the luggage van. Mission accomplished. (It is an unwritten rule of the clash of the cargo men that once an article is inside the bogey, it cannot be offloaded.)

With peace of mind I watched the Paschim pull out of the platform at 11.30 a.m. that Saturday morning. I could go home now, relax and catch my flight to Delhi the next morning. I'd have enough time to make it from the airport to the station. In exactly twenty-three hours from now, I would be waiting for the arrival of the Paschim Express on Platform 6 at New Delhi Railway Station.

Well, I was not.

My early morning flight to Delhi was on time and all that, but I messed up the trip from south Delhi to the railway station. The roads in the capital are very unforgiving: one turn missed and the poor motorist has to battle traffic and signals for at least a kilometre and a half before making a U-turn. This was my plight, riding pillion with an acquaintance who claimed to know the concrete jungle of Delhi as well as Jim Corbett knew the forests of the Kumaon. A presumptuous claim to say the least—had the latter's knowledge been as minuscule as the former's, old Jim would have ended up as a very tasty snack for the first man-eater that crossed his path.

The result was that I got to the platform panting from exhaustion at 10.45 a.m. and the Paschim had come, waited, tooted its merry horn and left—with my bike still on it, I assumed. There was one bike that they had unloaded, the luggage clerk told me, but that was a Bajaj Scooter. I asked him if he'd seen my bike inside and had forgotten to unload it, but he was clueless. I went into full panic mode. The Paschim must have made numerous stops between Mumbai and Delhi—where was I going to go looking for my motorcycle?

The clerk tried reassuring me. 'Don't worry,' he said, 'if it has been offloaded anywhere else it will be loaded on a train to Delhi, and if it's still on the train then it will be offloaded at the last stop, Amristar, and then be sent back. It may take five days to a week, but it'll reach without fail.' These railway chaps didn't seem to understand that the whole point of sending the motorcycle by train was to get it to Delhi within twenty-four hours; if it was going to turn into a weeklong saga that tested the networking of the Indian railways, I would have ridden it up to Delhi in three days.

I ran up the stairs of the overhead bridge, across five platforms and down the staircase and then sprinted the last hundred metres to the Parcels Department. There was no one there and the main office was bolted and locked with a Godrej Navtal (eight levers).

All this was starting to become uncomfortably familiar. Four years before, I'd arrived on the Golden Temple Mail at this very station with my bike in the luggage van, and even though it was unloaded on time, I had to grease every palm from the loaders to the clerks to the superintendent of luggage to the ticket collector at the gate to get my bike off the platform and out of the station. And that had been with my bike in sight. So harrowing had this experience been, that on my return, I had cancelled my train ticket and ridden back to Mumbai.

I feared that, this time, it was going to be far worse. My bike could either be languishing in a station in Gujarat, Madhya Pradesh or Rajasthan, or was as yet on the train speeding north at 120kmph. I winced as I thought of the trail of tips I'd be leaving behind and the maze of red tape I would have negotiated by the time I was reunited with my motorcycle. I was going to be days behind schedule, I'd have to shuttle between the station and south Delhi innumerable times, and—most disheartening—my finances were going to take a crippling blow. Like hyenas gathering around a dying animal, the loaders, clerks, superintendents and guards were going to move in to make my unfortunate inconvenience their monetary gain.

And it started with a sweeper. Seeing me staring woebegone at the locked door of the Parcels Department, he asked me who I was looking for and I blurted out my sad tale to him. 'Follow me,' he said, and I thought, *Here we go*. I remembered that I had all my cash in five hundred-rupee notes and made a mental note to change some into smaller denominations now that I would have to start handing out tokens of my heartfelt appreciation for services rendered.

The sweeper's name was Deepak and he led me to a

small shack just next to the luggage department. Inside were nine men, all sleeping. They were the loaders who had unloaded the Paschim, he told me. Deepak shook one of them awake and he confirmed that the bike was on the train, but because it was too heavy and there was too much luggage around, they hadn't been able to unload it in time. So now at least I knew that the bike was still on the train.

Deepak then led me to another office where the railway superintendent of luggage was sitting. Since he had to get back to work, he bid me goodbye and good luck. I stood waiting for the chai-paani request to come. It didn't.

There were five railway babus sitting and chatting over cups of tea. They listened to my problem with the sombreness of a tribunal at a court-martial hearing and then told me that the luggage clerk was right about the procedure; that was the protocol that would have to be followed, and I would just have to wait.

As I was walking out of the anteroom, the youngest of the five babus came up to me and told me that perhaps the people at the NR Cell could help me out but only the next day; today being a Sunday, they'd be shut. As an afterthought, he snapped his fingers and said that he had seen one of the officers in the morning and maybe the office was open after all. He took me to his office, put a call across and confirmed that the NR office was indeed open.

That office was at the other end of the platform, a six hundred-metre walk, and sitting there was a smartly-dressed young man chatting on the phone. He gestured for me to take a seat and finished his call. His name was Kapil.

'We're closed today, but I came in because I had to finish some work. How can I help you?' he asked. How many railway employees work overtime, I wondered, before pouring out my tale of woe for the fourth time. The events that followed bring a smile to my face to this day.

He asked me to relax, offered me water and despatched his peon to arrange tea for me. Then he pulled out the Paschim's schedule from his desktop computer. He opened a battered brown book that was the hotline directory to all stations in India and looked up and dialled Ambala Cantonment Railway Station. 'It's 11.45 now,' he told me, 'and the Paschim will arrive at Ambala at 2.15 p.m. We'll try to get your bike offloaded there.'

Praise the lord, here was a man of action rather than words. And mind you, he knew how to use his words too.

The NR Cell is in the upper echelons of the railway services, and railway employees at the station level take any call from there very seriously. And Kapil exploited this power to the full. As soon as he raised Ambala Cant., he asked to be connected to the luggage department. The operator on the other end must have replied that there was no one answering the extension and that he should call back later. Kapil explained that this was a matter of utmost urgency and that he would hold on while the luggage clerk was located. Five minutes later, when the clerk came on line, my new-found friend asked him his name and designation and explained the scenario to him. He gave him precise details of the bill ticket number, the location of the luggage bogey and the registration number of the motorcycle, and instructed him to offload the bike from the Paschim and load it into the 1058 Amritsar Dadar Express that would pull into Ambala Cant. at 3.25 p.m. He was to inform New Delhi as soon as this was done.

After hanging up with Ambala, he called the luggage clerk on the platform of New Delhi station where the 1058 would arrive at 8.05 p.m. and instructed him to offload the motorcycle.

Since there was nothing further I could do, I thanked Kapil and left.

When I returned to the station at 7.30 p.m., Kapil had left and in his place was Rattan. He told me that Kapil had apprised him of the matter but regretfully there had been no call from Ambala and he really didn't know if the bike had been loaded on the train.

Now Rattan was a Bullet owner too, and soon we

were talking motorcycles, faults, kinks, pistons, lubrication and rides. He was very excited by the fact that I was riding to Leh all by myself and we generally hit it off very well and I almost forgot my anxiety. We sauntered out of his office to the dhabas that lie between the station and Paharganj. Besides the common motorcycle, we also shared a taste for trotters in spicy gravy and Rattan took me through a maze of shops and restaurants to one that he swore served the best in all of Delhi. After we consumed his complete stock of trotters, the old Muslim cook anxiously waited for us to burp in satisfaction and then, when we did, broke into a toothy smile and served kesar phirni on the house.

Back in the NR Cell at 9 p.m., Rattan once again called Ambala and this time managed to get hold of the luggage clerk who was unwinding in that station's cafeteria. The clerk confirmed that he had followed instructions but hadn't managed to get through to Delhi on the phone. We rushed to the luggage department and sure enough, standing there packed and proud amongst other various-shaped boxes of cargo, was my motorcycle. It had been unloaded from the 1058 at 8.15 p.m. The office that issues the gate pass was closed, but again Rattan managed to locate the concerned clerk and requested him to come down to his office. The clerk then obliged by opening the office and clearing the paperwork so I could take my motorcycle that night and not have to return the next morning.

Rattan even siphoned out some fuel from his scooter to give me enough to get to the nearest petrol pump.

Instead of a week, my bike was returned to me in less than twelve hours; the sweeper Deepak, the babu at the luggage department, Kapil and Rattan had all made an extra effort to help me and had succeeded in mobilising people and reuniting me with my bike in record time. And not one of them had asked for chai-paani.

Good Friends and Biker Buddies

The next morning I started on my journey. Despite what my paranoia on the platform might indicate, I'm not really strait-jacketed by schedule, but this was a trip I'd dreamed about doing for over a decade. I knew I had to get to Srinagar via Leh in fifteen days. Two weeks on the road with my bike and my camera. For these two weeks, I would be a nomad, not even letting my head dictate terms. For this fortnight, I would follow my heart.

My bike, on the other hand, seemed to have problems following the direction of its front wheel. For all its size, voluptuous design and weight, the Bullet is still a very well balanced motorcycle; it is nimble in traffic and fluid around corners. That day, though, it was behaving like a ponderous pachyderm with a litre of local anaesthesia shot into its butt. I realised that I had packed too much. My luggage was sitting over the rear axle and compressing the rear shock absorbers to their maximum travel. If it was posing a problem on the straight roads out of Delhi, I knew that on the twisty hill roads of the Himalayas, my luggage would weigh my bike down like a ball and chain. Some serious jettisoning and repacking needed to be done. I decided to do this at my friends' place in Chandigarh.

I had been riding for an hour or so when Haryana's first thunderstorm of the season exploded right over me after Panipat. I went from bone dry to dripping wet in exactly forty-seven seconds. There wasn't even time for me to get my rain gear out. One moment it had been hot and sticky, and the next the thunderstorm had exploded as if a hydro dam had burst. As the water soaked in through my shoes and started collecting around my toes, I knew I had to stop and save my wallet and my phone from the deluge. I turned into the gate of what looked like a warehouse, blissfully ignoring the 'Trespassers will be prosecuted' sign, and out rushed the solitary chowkidar with a lathi in one hand and umbrella in the other. The fourth and fifth buttons of his khaki uniform were in a state of siege against the man's generous belly, and with every bounding step he took towards me, the buttons strained a little more as they tried to contain the bulge.

But above the magnificent belly lay a magnanimous heart, and the man took pity on my dishevelled state. He asked me to park the bike in the shed beside the guard room and then invited me in. He poured out tea from a thermos flask so grubby that I couldn't even figure out its original colour. The cup he handed me was chipped and the handle was missing. But the tea was hot, sweet and just what I needed to gather my wits again. It is random acts of kindness like this that make fond memories of road trips in India.

I stopped to sort my luggage out at my friends' Navaz and Karandip's home in Chandigarh. Their super-speed dryer had my clothes stiff and dry in little less than an hour. Karandip also lent me his vintage but superb riding glasses—the kind bikers and aviators wore in the 1940s. So with my luggage reduced and rearranged, and a final cup of their maid Karuna's divine cardamom tea, I set off towards Shimla just as afternoon was giving way to evening.

With my twenty-kilo load reduced to twelve, I hit the hills at Parwanoo, and to my relief my Bullet was quite compliant around the curves. The road to Shimla—NH 22—is quite the biker's delight, with wide corners and smooth surfaces. I spent the night in Shimla at the home of a couple I'd first met when they were on their honeymoon in Dandeli, Karnataka. Ruchi and Aarsh had come rafting with me on the Tons after that and we'd become good friends.

The next day I started off from Shimla and rode eighty kilometres to Thanedar where I have a very dear friend, Mr Thakur Prakash. Thakur Saab runs the very charming Banjara Orchard Retreat in Thanedar, and I consider it one of the best places to stay in all of the Himalayas. The rooms and log huts are very cosy, the food is delicious and Thakur Saab is a gracious host, full of stories and always ready for an invigorating trek. It has been nine years since I first met Thakur Saab, and in the course of driving to various parts of Himachal Pradesh, I've inevitably ended up spending a day or two in Thanedar. All I need to do is make a phone call and Thakur Saab ensures that there is a hot meal and a cosy bed ready for me.

I spent two relaxed days there before I started off towards the Jalori Pass, the first of the ten high-altitude passes I would have to cross before I rode into the vale of Kashmir.

The sun was shining when I started off from Thanedar at 4 p.m., but by the time I reached Khanag a few kilometres short of the Jalori Pass, the heavens opened up. The road, which had already made the going dodgy because of the number of potholes, became worse as all the dry mud turned to slush. The cold wind blowing off the hillsides through the trees sounded like the howls of a banshee in distress and I started getting a little worried. Not because of the winds or the gloomy ambience that the dark thunderclouds had created, but because my bike was now struggling for grip. The final stretch of the incline to the Jalori is very steep. When I tried to climb it in second gear, the engine knocked in alarm, as if it were telling me to stop being ridiculous and shift back into the first. The slush on the road ensured that the rear wheel had its own little tiff to sort out with traction. At every hairpin I'd try to keep the throttle open and not touch the clutch in an effort to keep momentum around the bend, but the slippery surface would send the bike sliding alarmingly to the edge of the road. I was just about coping with all these hostilities when, to my horror, a kilometre from the summit, a huge Himalayan Griffon vulture landed right in front of me, hissing and grunting. I was horrified, because vultures seem to know when a living being is going to die; they arrive to wait and feed on the carrion.

And now with this vulture in front of me, its yellow eyes gleaming with the evil stare of the devil himself, I wondered if it was my time to pass on. But then I realised that I was far too uncomfortable to even pass wind, let alone pass on. So I gave the bird a birdie, slammed the bike into the first gear, opened the throttle wide, let out the clutch and roared up to the Jalori, promising myself I'd die another day.

The hot tea at the little tea shop on the summit of the Jalori made for a good break, but I didn't get too comfortable as my destination was five kilometres ahead at Shoja. There's a retreat in the middle of this charming little village, surrounded by looming mountains on three sides. There were three jolly Sikh lawyers from Hoshiarpur visiting too, and they promptly invited me to their makeshift barbecue bar by a roaring bonfire. All of them, now in their mid-fifties, had travelled around northern India on Enfield motorcycles in their youth. So I sat with my new-found biker buddies, the fire banishing the chill in my bones and Old Monk warming my insides, as they plied me with chicken tikka and reminisced about their 'Bulleting' days.

Respect the Road

The Tirthan valley, which stretches from Shoja to Banjar and Gushaini, is just too beautiful to ride away from after a single day, so I decided to hang about, trekking to the Sewalsar lake five kilometres from Jalori Pass, fishing in the Tirthan river and picking fruits with the village kids.

I ended up staying four days in the valley, spending time in Banjara Retreat in Shoja, the Himalayan Trout House in Nagini village, and Raju's Cottage in Gushaini. Finally I left the Tirthan river behind, crossed over the Beas on the bridge at Aut, where I joined the

Chandigarh-Manali road. Aut is seventy kilometres from Manali and I roared into Manali close to noon.

From late May to early September, the thump of the Bullet's single cylinder engine is the very soundtrack of Manali. It is a cherished dream of most Bullet owners to do the classic Manali to Leh ride. A sort of pilgrimage or initiation into the cult that is 'Bulleting'. So there are plenty of Bullets in Manali during these months, some with number plates from as far away as Maharashtra, Karnataka, Goa and Kerala. The local mechanics are experts in servicing Bullets and preparing them for the arduous road ahead, and I got my bike serviced here. The rear brakes had taken a fair share of wear and tear, and the setting of the clutch had to be readjusted. Happy that my bike was in tip-top shape to take on the road ahead, I spent a relaxed evening and night in Manali and the next morning started off towards the high road to Leh.

I still remember the time when Chetan and I had taken on this very road in August 2001, cocky and arrogant, confident that our Gypsy, Maruti's very capable off-roader, would take anything the road threw at it. The Gypsy did, but we didn't. We ascended too high, too fast and AMS hit us hard. Sunburn, nausea, headaches and an overwhelming sense of gloom that we were going to perish are all morbid memories of that first traverse. And we had received fair warning in

Manali from an old Buddhist monk. Advice that we'd scoffed at.

The story of that first ascent to Leh from Manali is in this verse that I wrote after that terrible drive.

To a land called Ladakh we were preparing to go,
Over high roads generously peppered with snow.
The old monk saw us packing the car and a greeting he waved,
Which I returned since I am moderately well-behaved.

'So you're off to my land of Ladakh I guess,
It will take you two days to reach at best.'
'No sir, I have a very capable car, you see,
And within a day in the city of Leh we'll be.'

'Yes son, the car will handle the road, that is true,
What I'm wondering is whether or not will you.
Those roads are high and almost touch the sky
It would be prudent to be a little shy.'

And, worrying his beads, he walked away with a limping gait,
And I scoffed at his warning—I was in good physical shape.
It was a terrible mistake I made,
And the price in full I paid.

We climbed that towering road too high and too quick,
And at the fifteen thousand-foot high Baralacha La fell violently sick.

Altitude mountain sickness had enveloped me in a deadly embrace,
My head hurt, my stomach retched, and around me the world
reeled at a furious pace.

Had to make Sarchu, the only sheltered place to stay,
And it was misery personified every kilometre of the way.

Mountains and streams make Sarchu a place of unimaginable beauty,
But appreciating it was beyond me as I lay groaning, nauseous and retchy.
It could have been paradise for all I care,
Inside my mind it was the devil's lair.

The gentle monk had tried to warn us,
Words that I'd dismissed as an old man's fuss.
Here in the mountains where altitude is king,
Hurry or haste is a very deadly thing.

A million times I called to my God that night,
And then I saw the bright shining light.

I snapped awake shivering with fear; are the angels here, is my end near?
'Not yet, my son,' a voice seemed to say in my ear.
It was the sun shining through the tent, the beginning of another day,
My head felt good and I could stand without feeling the world sway.

That remains my most distressing night,
Those seven hours that I took to fight the height.
I am wiser now and whenever that awesome road I drive,
I remember the monk and am never in a hurry to arrive.

Apart from AMS, I'd been instantly humbled by the Manali-Leh road: it demands fear and respect and it doesn't give you very many second chances. Which is why I joined up with a few other riders also heading towards Leh. Camaraderie is prevalent on the road to Leh, especially if you're on a motorcycle. If you're sitting by your bike with your head in your hands, other bikers will most certainly stop and enquire if all's well. And it's a long and hard ride, especially if you're alone, so when I met a group of riders at the mechanic's place, we'd gotten talking and I decided to ride with them to Leh.

The fifty-kilometre long and winding road to the Rohtang Pass should have been a splendid start for the 480 kilometre ride, given its smooth tarred surfaces, chequered landscapes and the cold, crisp, invigorating mountain air. But it was not to be. It was Saturday morning and holidaymakers who had come to spend the weekend in Manali were rushing towards Rohtang for a day trip. The volume of traffic that narrow road was subjected to soon translated into traffic jams and clouds of exhaust fumes. The acrid smell of burning clutches soon rent the air as our heavily-loaded Bullets dodged traffic and climbed the steep inclines.

Rohtang Pass was chaos personified. There were Lajjos from Ludhiana and Paajis from Patiala with Buntys from Bilaspur and Jollys from Jalandhar. Scrawny ponies valiantly carried fat aunties with rear ends as sprawling as Rashtrapati Bhavan, honeymooners posed for posterity and hyper kids were being chased by mortified mummies trying to get them to wear their sweaters.

Leaving Rohtang behind was like accelerating from gloom to paradise. As we descended, on the other side, the fog cleared and the views got better. Our forearms, aching from the constant working of the clutch and brake levers, got a chance to recover on this empty road. As a result, the first-timers in the group assumed the ride up to Rohtang was the worst of it and were soon thinking, 'Hah! I can tame this road'. The little streams we encountered were crossed in style. Some riders even rode to and fro several times so that their heroics could be captured on film. At the night halt in Darcha, everyone was in high spirits; loud jokes flew across the table and the laughter was infectious. As I took in the happy scene around me, I couldn't help but wonder what it would be like twenty-four hours from now. To the north, the snow on Baralacha La shone like a beacon—it was there that high altitude sickness would raise its ugly head.

The next morning, before we set off, most riders—clad in thermals and jackets—popped Disprin and Diamox, comforting themselves in the belief that the little pills would protect them against altitude sickness. As I rode up the road to Baralacha La, I came across clusters of snow sporadically; it became more frequent the higher I got. After a certain height, the roadsides were still snow-logged and the path had been cleared by a snow cutter. Barren mountainsides with caps of dazzling white snow now dominated the views. The first headaches started near Baralacha La; the 16,600-

foot high altitude was making its presence known. I was now riding at an altitude higher than the maximum limit for commercial skydiving—15,000 feet.

Then we came across a section where the river had changed course and was now flowing on the road for about 800 metres. This was, by any standards, a tough one—it made the streams we had crossed earlier look like trickles. By the time we manoeuvred through, most of the bikers I was riding with were a sorry sight. Shoes soaked with icy-cold water, hands wrinkled and numb.

But worst off were the bikers within the group who'd had an hour-long picnic atop Baralacha La—a big mistake! It gave AMS enough time to breach the Disprin-Diamox fortification and tighten its grip on them. Headaches cropped up like mushrooms in a forest after a rainy day. Craniums throbbed and stomachs retched as AMS ruled, and the cold afternoon winds added to the misery.

The inside of the parachute tent in Sarchu that miserable second night had the deathlike stillness of a morgue. Some riders were so exhausted that they had collapsed on the thick cotton mattresses still dressed in their dust- and sand-covered riding gear. Those who'd made the effort to pull off their riding gear and take their luggage off their bikes realised that the exertion was bringing on a fresh attack of nausea and headaches.

Riders like me, who hadn't lingered at the summit of Baralacha La, were fine that evening in Sarchu. We sat around a little bonfire nursing small measures of rum, trying to spot various constellations in the sparkling sky.

The next morning, most of the riders were back to normal with just a few residual headaches, which the crisp morning air and breakfast soon dissolved. Scorn was out, humility was in. We still had two high-altitude passes to go. But the Baralacha La lesson had been well learned: no rider spent more than five minutes at either the Lachung La or the Tanglang La.

Riding down from Tanglang La to Upshi was a blast. The freshly-laid roads lent a renewed twist to the wrist and the Ladakh range echoed with the staccato sound of twelve Bullets racing towards the restaurant in Rumste, where a soldier from south India mans the world's highest idli-dosa joint.

Leh!

This little city perched at 11,000 feet welcomes all those who come to it with the promise of laidback days and easy evenings. The narrow window of hospitality that Leh offers, because of its location at the roof of the world, is from June to the middle of October. It is then that Leh is vibrant with visitors and buzzing with small businesses. The town literally comes alive with quaint little restaurants with menus which imaginatively spell the same dishes very differently every year. After four visits to Leh, my favourite still remains the German Bakery on Library Road. Run by three or four cheerful brothers from Punjab, the place has a nice feel to it. The German Bakery is a place where you'd want to have your hearty morning breakfast before you start a long day of exploring the city and its surroundings. You can choose from piping hot porridge and pancakes to freshly baked bread and a range of teas. But these teas mean tea bags with delicate flavours and subtle tastes—camomile, mint or cardamom. A more adventurous type may choose ginger. These are teas meant to be had with just hot water; sugar or honey is allowed with a slight frown from the purists, but milk is absolute sacrilege. I have never been able to acquire a taste for this—what I consider—degradation of tea. Tea is meant to be strong and dark, with a dash of milk and sugar and spice. And preferably a biscuit by the side. Thankfully the proprietors of the German Bakery empathise with people like me, so there is aromatic masala chai on the menu as well.

The Bike Bandit

After a few easy days in Leh, I set off towards Srinagar, riding alone once again. I'd been with the group of bikers for almost a week, and that morning, riding all alone on the narrow road out of Leh, loneliness shrouded me. The feeling was enhanced by the landscape: central Leh is busy and vibrant, and it is only on the outskirts that one gets a true feel of how expansive and desolate Ladakh can be.

The towering mountains, the vastness around me, all of it made me very aware of my mortality. Amidst the immensity of this place, where everything around me could be dated in ages and millennia, my entire life seemed just a blink of an eye. A rock precariously balanced on a cliff edge had probably been there decades before I was born and would remain there long after I was dead. If I missed a corner and went off the road, down a sheer drop, the subsequent effort to recover my body would be so great, they'd probably let me lie there and place a small memorial plaque at the edge of the road. Like the ones I had seen already on this ride.

I realised that these morbid thoughts were weighing me down, so I wiped my mind clean of them like one sweeps clutter off a desk, and looked at the pros. My bike was singing sweetly and rhythmically, the luggage had been packed well and was perfectly balanced, and the roads were baby-bottom smooth. I was able to make Kargil, 222 kilometres away, in five hours, even after a quick stop to visit the Lamaruyu monastery which is 111 kilometres from Leh. At Kargil, I checked into Hotel De Zoji La.

Kargil still has the air of an old frontier town and my Bullet, with its Maharashtra number plate, was immediately noticed. A few local lads came up to me when I was having my usual post-ride cup of chai at a local tea stall and started a conversation. I realised that Mumbai held as much wonder for them as the cities in Europe do for me. They asked me questions like, 'Have you met Amitabh Bachchan', 'Have you seen Aishwarya Rai', 'If I come to Mumbai will I find a job easily'.

One of them, not quite as enamoured by film stars, was eyeing my bike with keen interest. He asked me whether I had bought it brand new and what it was worth now. So I told him that I'd bought it in 1998 and it would probably be worth about Rs 50,000 now.

That evening, at around 9 p.m., after I'd had a bath, eaten my dinner and was finishing off some accounts to see whether my funds would outlive my trip, someone knocked on my door. It was the one of the lads from my tea shop banter—the one who'd asked me about my bike.

He was with a bearded man who seemed to be his father or uncle or some family elder—the sort who didn't take too kindly to an argument. Without preamble he started off by saying, 'My boy likes your bike and I am buying it from you for him. As you'd agreed with him regarding the price, here is Rs 50,000 in cash.'

I was taken aback to say the least. I tried to slide a sentence in sideways to explain that I hadn't implied my bike was for sale when the boy had asked me its worth. But it was like trying to talk back to a public loudspeaker. He was the kind of man who spoke in declarations and sentences that rang with finality. I don't think he was used to someone disagreeing with him.

I was trying to get to the end of my first sentence—which largely consisted of negations and denials—but before I made it to the full stop, Mr Loudspeaker had piled five bundles of currency on the little rickety table in my room. I doggedly tried to explain once again that the bike was not for sale, which he perceived as bargaining banter and added another bundle to the pile.

A slimy python of fear started uncoiling in my stomach. The plastic bag that he was pulling out currency bundles from still had a promising bulge, so, instead of arguing with him and having him pile more and more money in my little room, which was already starting to look like a safe deposit locker, I told him I'd like to think over the final price and give him an answer in the morning. They then went on to insist that I keep Rs 10,000 as a 'good intention deposit', which I managed to avoid saying that I didn't feel safe keeping so much money in this hotel room with a door that didn't lock properly. They finally left saying they'd be back at eight the next morning.

I waited for forty-five minutes after they'd left and then started packing furiously. I stealthily took my luggage down, and as quietly as possible loaded it onto my bike. I didn't want anybody to see me. If the lad and his father (or whoever) had located me right to my hotel room in Kargil, I was sure that news about me making moves to hightail it out of Kargil would get to them in a jiffy.

I winced at the roar of my bike as it came to life in half a kick; I felt like the exhaust's snarl must have been heard all over Kargil. And on cue a few lights came on in the hotel. The manager poked his head out of his window on the first floor and then I saw him reach for the phone. Positive that he was calling the bearded man, I leapt onto my Bullet with alacrity, opened the throttle wide and let out the clutch too rapidly. As a result of which the engine stalled, and since the throttle was wide open, the carburettor flooded.

I rapidly kicked the bike, more panicky with every passing moment, till my right leg was fatigued. I looked up to see a light come on in another room of the hotel—and who should poke his head out the window but the bearded man himself!

He looked down at me and froze, then snarled and disappeared inside. I knew that he was on his way down. As if on cue to the thought, I heard a door slam deep inside the hotel and heavy feet started stomping down the stairs.

'Please, please start,' I begged my bike. My knees were knocking together—the right from fatigue and the left from fear. The bike responded with a hesitant sputter and then died again. The stomping was now louder than ever and the man burst out of the building and started walking up to me shouting, 'Where are you going? We have a deal!'

He was six feet away when I shoved the bike off the stand and started pushing it towards the gate of the hotel.

'Watchman, stop him!' shouted the man.

I looked at the man being called and thanked God for the fact that the watchman fit the stereotype, which meant that he had his head thrown back and mouth open in deep slumber. I rushed past him as he groggily stood up and I shoved him back in the chair with a firm fist in the chest. He leapt up again, still not fully awake, and this time grabbed the bearded man who was rushing past him in pursuit of me. The bearded man furiously boxed the watchman on his ears shouting, 'Catch *him*, catch *him*, you silly old fool; not me!'

In the six seconds it took the man to disentangle himself from the watchman's zealous grip, I had stretched my lead to about fifteen feet. I leapt onto the bike and shifted it into second gear. The man who was now huffing and puffing behind me, his kurta pyjama flapping in the wind, had his hand outstretched and was rapidly closing the distance between us. In a second or two at the most he would be grabbing my neck. I let out the clutch, willing my motorcycle to start. The Bullet sputtered angrily, died and then instantly caught again with a roar just as his fingers were brushing the nape of my neck. I opened the throttle wide and the bike responded beautifully this time, shooting ahead truly like a bullet from a gun. I looked back to see the bearded man, his face dark with rage and exertion, panting hard with one hand on his chest and the other balled in a fist which he was waving at me.

God Bless Mrs Abraham and Sawant Rao Joshi

I roared out of Kargil shivering with fright at my near escape. My bike was not for sale, not for fifty grand nor a lakh, and that bearded bandit could go buy a horse or a house with his fortune—he wasn't going to get my bike!

Little did I realise that my adventures were far from over. I'd started off from Kargil at 11.25 p.m. That nocturnal ride has been my most harrowing journey ever. The road was tarmac at some places but dirt at most others. Luckily, I'd had a halogen bulb installed in my headlight before this Himalayan trip, and now the strong beam caught the large rocks in my path so I was able to avoid them. I have never, ever seen darkness like that, not before that night and not after. I couldn't see anything beyond the throw of my headlight.

It is during that night somewhere on the road between Kargil and Drass that my fondness for my bike turned into lifelong love. I was never more dependent on it as I was at that time. Its steady thump—loud, proud, unfaltering and reassuring—boosted my confidence. It was as if, with every note its mud-caked cylinder sent out through its short chrome exhaust, it was telling me, *Let this road throw anything at us, we'll ride through it.* Over roads strewn with glacier moraine, across dark streams that shimmered in my headlight beam, through broken tarmac and soft muddy slush, my Bullet responded beautifully to the twist of my wrist. I got to Drass at a little past two in the morning.

In this little village—where the temperature fell to 60 degrees Centigrade on Monday, the ninth of January 1995—a solitary tea shop was open. In it there was a wizened old man, whose beard was just short of his navel, tending a contraption that looked like an ancient bathroom geyser. It was hissing, bubbling and squeaking like my stomach had during the incident with the full cream milk on the Uttar Pradesh-Haryana border. It was an ancient tea percolator, possibly left behind by the khansama of Babur's army. The tea he poured out was flavoured with cinnamon, saffron and cardamom and sweetened with honey. It seemed to seek out and eliminate the chill in my bones and weeded out the weariness in my muscles.

I realised my arms and forearms were in a state of fixed flex from gripping the handlebars tight. The hot tea within the beautifully tapered glass I cupped in my hands warmed and comforted me. Sipping on it, I felt hope—I had made it till Drass, and I would make it to Srinagar. It would be alright.

It was the chai walla who solemnly broke the news that felt like an avalanche of doom and despair collapsing on me. When I told him that I was on my way to Srinagar, he said, 'It is Friday today—dry day.'

Now dry day there doesn't mean that the local watering hole will be serving only orange juice and Virgin Marys. It means that the mighty Zoji La, the dramatic mountain pass that separates Ladakh from Kashmir, is closed by the Indian army. Fridays are when they carry out routine maintenance of the pass, clearing landslides and repairing broken stretches.

Now this was during the time when cross-border firing was routine and Drass got its share of direct hits. The kind old chai walla pointed out Drass's best guest house to me. I looked across at it and brought up the obvious—that half of it was reduced to a pile of rubble.

'Oh, that half took a glancing blow from a shell last evening, but there are still some perfectly undamaged rooms. You can stay the day there today and leave tomorrow, or you can ride back to Kargil and come back again tomorrow.'

Neither option was very inviting. A slight adjustment to the scope of his howitzer and the enemy gunner could finish the other half of the guesthouse to make it a very symmetrical pile of rubble. And, back at Kargil, Mr Moneybags was possibly already gathering a posse of locals to chase after my bike.

I decided I would rather take my chances with the pass.

So once again I headed out into the night, where the only world visible to me was what fell within the circle of light thrown by my Bullet's headlamp. After I passed Meena Marg I saw the first vehicles since I'd left Kargil. They were all parked there and would start for Srinagar, over the pass, on Saturday, the next morning. I carried on. A few called out saying that the pass was closed and I wouldn't be allowed beyond the Gumri check-post a few kilometres ahead, but I ignored them.

At Gumri, the barrier was down but there wasn't anyone in sight so I got off the bike, ducked under the barrier, hopped back on and carried on.

When I was in my teens, one of the most fascinating

films I saw was *The Great Escape*. Steve McQueen, who plays the Cooler King in the film, was the ultimate image of 'cool' for me. I had watched that sequence of him trying to escape the Germans on a captured motorcycle over and over again. Today I was living a shade of that role—as in I was a fugitive and maybe I hadn't jumped my bike over the barrier with the style and panache with which McQueen jumped over the barbed wire on the German-Swiss border, but I too was expecting a shrill whistle ordering me to stop and turn back. It never came.

At the second barrier, at the approach to the pass, a sentry was there, awake and alert, and he promptly ordered me to turn back and come again tomorrow.

It is my firm belief that if you've tried hard enough, Lady Luck will ride pillion with you. And I'd ridden a hard and difficult ride from Kargil to this spot, and so when my light caught the soldier's name tag, I knew I'd got my ticket across the pass. His name was Sawant Rao Joshi. He was from Maharashtra, and I suspected that, posted here in Kashmir, he was probably dying to parley in his mother tongue. So I sent up a silent prayer asking the Almighty to bless Mrs Abraham, my elementary school Marathi teacher who had practised her linguistic trade with the liberal use of a thick, foot-long wooden ruler which she had applied with great force and endeavour to my backside, and let out a jovial greeting in Marathi. Sawant Rao was ecstatic; he was from Pune and happily so was my motorcycle, which was registered in Pune.

Domicile bonding happened then and there. He ordered some tea from the little canteen, brought out his cherished stock of biscuits and Wills cigarettes and insisted that I spend some time there. After thoroughly checking all my documents he told me to ride fast and get across the crest of the pass. Once I'd crossed over and started going downhill I could take it easy, he said.

When I stopped at the summit of the Zoji La to get that all-important photograph, I tried to put down the side stand to rest my bike, but my foot couldn't find it. I looked down and realised that it had been sheared off its mount. Then I tried to engage the main stand but my foot couldn't find that either—it too had been sheared off its mounting plate. I realised that some of the rocks I had ridden over had scraped the underbelly of my Bullet and it had taken a toll.

But it was a small price to pay. My bike had carried me over atrocious roads without a single puncture. I leaned the bike against the Zoji La milestone and got my photograph.

It was then that I met a shepherd who had been grazing his livestock on the sparse shrub that valiantly battles the harsh terrain. He had a little primus stove and was about to brew some tea which he offered to share with me. The milk, of course, was going to come straight from a goat. I was very well aware of what the ramifications of tea with 'direct from source' milk could be, but I was so tired and so exuberant after having conquered the road from Kargil to Zoji La through the night without any untoward incident, that I decided to have the tea. And, anyway, there was enough squatting room and isolation around if disaster did strike. Fortunately the tea went down well—I even had a second cup.

The shepherd had lived all his life roaming these hills and it was he who told me the interesting tale that follows. It was one of those stories that had been passed down from generation to generation—probably getting more fanciful with each telling.

Tenso Tanshin was extremely ticked off.

The tough Mongol had been obligated to take the route through Ladakh that summer of 1603 because his chieftain had requested him to do so. The chieftain wanted him to take some monks to the Lamaruyu monastery on the way to Central Europe. Usually Tenso and his caravan took the route through northern China on their way to Central Europe—Ladakh was a long detour to the south.

At first Tenso had tried to reason with the chief, telling him how it would upset his schedule, but the chief had solemnly snapped his fingers and an executioner with bulging biceps, black hood and bloodstained axe had instantly materialised in the room. The chief had made his request again then, even more politely and softly, with an ingratiating smile, and Tenso had agreed with alacrity.

Another thorn in Tenso's side was the dozen young Bactrian camels he thought he'd bought for a steal from the local tribesmen in the Nubra valley. He'd penned both sexes together so they could have a merry romp as often as they pleased and he would make a nice profit on his investment from the resulting offspring. But these darn double-humped beasts thought they were out on an exercise of abstinence. There had been no intermingling amongst the sexes. In fact, they were behaving as if they were out on a Sunday school picnic. All they were doing was happily munching through his livestock fodder. The sight of the male and female camels standing at a respectful distance from each other, constantly chewing cud with the satisfied expression of gastronomic bliss on their faces, had started to get on his nerves.

But more than his circuitous route and the herd of non-humping, humped quadrupeds, it was his bunch of fifty-seven merry wives that was really ticking him off. He'd chosen fourteen of the youngest—hourglass of figure and acquiescent of disposition—to take along and keep him company, but his older wives—thick of waist and shrill of voice—had insisted on coming along. Central Europe was a long and dangerous journey, and should anything happen to Tenso, the senior wives didn't want the younger ones getting their hands on his vast fortune. And now every morning, when it was time to break camp and move on, he fretted and fumed as his gaggle of wives were inevitably ready only when the sun was high in the sky.

He should have been in Turkey by now, and yet here he was, standing on the summit of Zoji La as his vivacious mates cackled and gossiped as they finally started the day's journey. Tenso cast a nervous glance at the huge cliffs of snow that hung above them, half scared that their high-pitched voices might start an avalanche and half-hoping that one would occur and bury all fifty-seven of them and cut out this cacophonic concert once and for all.

So yes, Tenso Tanshin was extremely ticked off as he descended from Zoji La, when suddenly he rounded a corner of the cobbled road and his anger and bitterness dissolved into joy and pleasure. His heart almost stood still as he shielded his eyes and looked heavenwards, wondering for a second whether his day of reckoning had come. How else could he explain the almost unbearable beauty in front of him? He galloped back and asked his wives to hurry up so they could see what he had, surprising them because this was the first time in many days that they'd seen a smile in his eyes.

Tenso Tanshin had just seen Sonamarg—the eastern gateway to Kashmir.

Whether this story that the shepherd told me was a bedtime tale or documented history, I don't know, but I'm sure one aspect of it is true, because four hundred years later, similar emotions rushed through me when I stood at the very same place looking down upon Sonamarg.

Of course, I didn't have a harrowing harem following me, nor was I plagued by unobliging camels; my troubles were restricted to apprehension and tiredness. I'd been riding my bike for over six hours, through the night, alone, on stark, desolate mountain roads. The sharp rocks I'd ridden over were very capable of blowing my tyres out, and that had fuelled my fear. Also, I was weary with the effort of swinging around the heavily-loaded bike, trying to avoid the worst of them.

But the sight of Sonamarg made all that vanish. With its rolling green meadows, pine-forested gentle slopes merging into lofty white caps, this oft ignored little hamlet was my first welcome to India's prettiest state. And though I've been to Kashmir many times since, it is that dawn view of Sonamarg from high above that flashes in my mind whenever I think of that state.

As I tucked into tea and breakfast sitting in a meadow at Sonamarg by the river Bind, I felt a sense of achievement. Though I still had to get to Srinagar and Jammu, I knew that the toughest roads were behind me. It would be regular highways from here on. The ride from Kargil to Sonamarg—just 190 kilometres—had taken me eight hours. I looked at my Bullet, coated with dust and the clayey grime that covered its engine and dulled its chrome. I couldn't help but feel an overwhelming sense of affection for it. I had overloaded and abused it, coaxed it up steep inclines, ridden it across many a river, demanded long hours in extreme conditions from it and all this across some of the toughest terrain in the world. But my motorcycle had shone through, never baulking or stuttering. It had done it all without a whimper.

Unbiased Bullet

I ran into my first traffic jam a few kilometres after Sonamarg, just before Gund. Two local buses had reached a deadlock in the middle of the narrow street and the drivers were now staring each other down, trying to will the other to back up with the intensity of their glares. In the meantime, traffic piled up behind each bus. Normally this would have been a hiccup in my ride, but after desolate roads with not a vehicle or a soul in sight, I revelled in this mess of motors and blowing horns. Besides, I was able to slip through because I was on a motorcycle.

I'd heard so much about Kashmir and the troubles that plagued the state that I expected to see tanks and battle troops at regular intervals. However, the road to Srinagar, and Srinagar itself, were surprisingly normal (this was in 2003). There were army men on patrol at regular intervals, but people were out everywhere— youngsters zipped around on motorcycles, couples walked hand-in-hand on the promenade by the lake. This was just like any other city. In fact, because of the usual cacophony that a city emanates, it was a little jarring. I parked my bike in the main parking lot at Nehru Park by Dal lake and called the houseboat I had booked from Leh. The boat's man Friday, Riyaz, answered and told me that he'd be by the pier with his shikara in ten minutes to row me across.

While I was waiting at the pier with my bags and my biking paraphernalia, including my helmet, balaclava, scarf, jacket and riding goggles, school children passing by kept looking at me, whispering and laughing. I looked at myself in the side view mirror of a parked auto-rickshaw and realised that my face was black except for the part that the goggles had covered. I looked quite a sight, like a First World War pilot who had just about managed to walk away alive from his downed bi-plane.

Riyaz arrived and helped me load my luggage onto the shikara. He had to park the long boat sideways to facilitate the transfer of my bags and in doing so he found himself flush against the pier with other arriving shikaras blocking his way out into the lake. Kashmiri is a tongue of the mountains and it is such a sweet language that, to an outsider like me, even the most vitriolic verbal duel sounds like an enthusiastic love song. I realised this after Riyaz—trying to negotiate his shikara from its place at the wide-stepped tier—knocked a fellow shikara walla into the water by mistake.

I spent five days in Srinagar, exploring the city or just floating down the lake on a shikara. My houseboat, Dastaan, was palatial, with one suite and four deluxe rooms, each with its own attached bathroom. By the end of my third day aboard, some kind of routine had been established to my mornings. First Riyaz and I would go shopping on the lake, visiting the baker, the butcher and the florist. Then we'd row across to the promenade, tie our shikara and buy a newspaper, which I would then read on the portico of the houseboat. At 7.30, Kareem, the laundry man, would row along to deliver or collect clothes. Hardly would the wake of his boat settle than old bearded Faiyaz would row in from the west and try to convince me to buy his saffron. I think he'd realised on the first day itself that I wasn't a likely customer, but the dear old man was full of stories of his youth in the Northwest Frontier Province, so I'd invite him onto the houseboat to have a cup of tea and he was happy to regale someone with tales of the 'good old days'.

My fourth day there happened to be a Monday. Though Chashma Shahi and Pari Mahal, two of Srinagar's prime tourist attractions that have a common access, are closed on Mondays, I had a special permit from the tourism department which allowed me a brief visit.

As I stood by the entrance to Chashma Shahi, waiting for the very stern-looking Rajput jawan to finish examining the permit, I could hear the strains of Daler Mehndi fill the air. '*Tunuk tunuk taa naa naa*' was getting louder by the second, and then around the corner came a Toyota Qualis, stuffed to the gills with tourists from Punjab with turbans in a variety of colours— enough to make a rainbow disappear in shame.

The harrowed taxi driver was squashed against the car door, with barely enough room to work the gearshift and the steering wheel, as the high-spirited sardars kept the combined decibel level of music and conversation hovering at 125 decibels—enough to rival an Iron Maiden concert.

The Rajput jawan was not at all happy at this sudden onslaught of Punjabi-pop, parathas and papajis. Yet he politely told the tourists, who were now sticking their heads out of the window, that the attraction was closed today and they would have to come back tomorrow if they wanted to see it.

They wouldn't listen, however, and kept trying to cajole him into letting them inside. They sweet-talked him and tried tempting him with parathas and pedhas, which he politely refused and yet again requested that they leave at once. The persistent lot wouldn't take no for an answer and I could see that the army man was starting to lose his patience. Finally, one of the tourists from within the depths of the car called out, 'Oye yaar. We've come all the way from Punjab, let us go in and have a quick look around. What difference will it make?'

The jawan had had enough. He believed in 'yes' or 'no', 'black' or 'white'; there was no room in his mind for 'maybe' or 'gray'. He had told this lot that the place was closed and yet they were standing there bargaining as if they were buying fruit and vegetables at Lal Chowk.

He meticulously folded my permit along its original creases and handed it back to me. He then gestured that I should go and stand behind him, which I did immediately, because it really doesn't make sense to argue with a man holding a loaded gun. He then un-shouldered his carbine, curled his finger around the trigger and said in a voice loaded with suggestion: 'Punjabi or Pakistani—my bullet doesn't regard race or nationality. It flies true to its target.' He pulled at a lever on the gun that made a loud click-clack sound which rang with ominous finality.

The poor driver, squashed like a patty between the

passengers and the door of the Qualis, finally snapped. At the sound of the cocking of the gun he reacted like a colt feeling the sting of a riding whip. He spun the Qualis round on its haunches with a squeal of rubber, causing a great deal of jostling within—I actually saw a paratha smeared with achaar fly out of a rear window—and accelerated away from the guard post.

Daler Mehedi, who was still stuck on 'Tunuk tunuk taa naa naa', faded away as the car disappeared out of sight. All that remained was acrid blue tyre smoke that hung in the air and the paratha lying on the road where the Qualis had stood.

The jawan burst out laughing and I gave a few hesitant grins before requesting him to please uncock his gun and put it back on his shoulder.

The Pathan of Pahalgam

After I'd relaxed in Srinagar and shaken off the aches of my 2000-kilometre ride and the feeling had returned to my rear, I started off for Pahalgam.

It's a lovely ride from Pahalgam to Anantnag on NH 1D. The famous Chinar trees line the roads and, at Pampur, saffron fields stretch to the horizon. Some of the world's best saffron grows here. The landscape gets even better from Anantnag to Pahalgam. Like Sonamarg, Pahalgam is also drop dead beautiful by virtue of its location. It is situated at the conjunction of a stream from the Shesh Nag lake and the Lidder river and all around are lofty snow-capped peaks.

In the five days I had spent in Kashmir, confidence in my personal safety had become so strong that I decided to set up my little tent on a grassy knoll by the river rather than be constrained within the confines of a room. In an attempt to take the whole 'back to nature' approach a step further, I even tried to get my own fire going. That is when Mohsin Khan stepped in. The shepherd had been passing by and stopped to watch my attempts to start a fire with mild curiosity. As dense clouds of smoke started to rise without the hint of a flame, his curiosity turned to concern. He quickly came and squatted next to me. He re-arranged the wood and took out some shavings from the cloth bag he was carrying and soon a crackling fire was going. I had wanted to make some tea and asked him to wait a while and have a cup with me. Mohsin Khan turned out to be a purist—he shook his head indulgently at tea bags and condensed milk.

'Son, you may as well go to a hotel and have tea. You've spent an hour getting this fire going and now you make shortcut tea on it. Not done!' he declared.

He pulled out a small penknife, slit open the teabags and sprinkled the tea leaves from within into water that was put on the boil. Out from the cloth bag came a glass bottle that was filled with milk and stoppered shut with a tapered piece of wood. My stomach involuntarily recoiled at the sight of milk from an unknown source. Mohsin Khan confirmed that it was from one of his buffaloes and that it had been boiled that morning before being bottled. He delved into the bag and out came a little leather pouch from which he drew a pinch of saffron, which he added to the tea.

He then covered the vessel and let it simmer for about ten minutes before pouring it out in a glass, adding a dollop of honey (again from the bag, which I was quite seriously beginning to consider enchanted) and handing it over to me. It was delicious. The aroma of saffron mingled with that of wood smoke and pine made it a delicious brew infused with unique flavour.

The old Pathan shepherd knew Pahalgam like the back of his hand, having spent all his sixty-seven years in the vicinity of the village. 'There Shammi Kapoor saab danced with Sharmila Tagore in *Kashmir ki Kali*,' he told me, pointing to a distant undulating slope beyond the river.

He was very pleasant company to spend the evening with, but his culinary skills were what made him especially endearing. I told him I planned to make some mutton that evening and he looked at me with mild surprise. His look seemed to say: you've been struggling to start a fire and you're going to attempt to cook mutton—a little ambitious, don't you think? But being the polite gentleman he was, he suggested instead that he would help me cook if I would like that. I was, of course, delighted to have some help.

We went and bought some mutton from a nearby butcher—Mohsin Khan firmly insisting that we buy a shank, rather than a rump as I had originally planned. He also asked for a part of the bone—more flavour and stock, you see! The thought of the meal that the old Pathan made that evening still makes my mouth water. It was a simple recipe that consisted of first sautéing cinnamon, bay leaves and red chillies in home-made ghee. Then in went the onions, crushed coriander seeds, cumin powder and a pinch of nutmeg. Once this spice mixture was cooked, Mohsin Khan added the meat and let it sizzle as the spices coated it. Once this whole meat and masala mixture had browned, he added very finely chopped tomatoes, some fresh coriander and a pinch of saffron. In went some fresh spring water which, to my surprise and—I must admit—horror, he drew straight from the Lidder river. The pot was covered and the meat allowed to cook over a slow flame for two hours. In the meantime, I rode to the local bakery and bought some of that famed Kashmiri sweet bread. Since we'd made more than we could eat, two of Mohsin Khan's grandchildren joined us. His entire clan was encamped on the other side of the Lidder.

That night was just two days short of a full moon, and by the time we'd finished dinner, the entire landscape was enveloped in a silvery-white shine. Mohsin Khan's grandchildren ran off to their settlement on the other side of the river and he sat with me, smoking his little portable hookah. Sitting by the river with the gurgle of his hookah competing with that of the river and the aromatic smoke wafting around me, it all suddenly seemed very clear why generations of Indians right from Emperor Ashoka to the common man today has cherished Kashmir. In my mellow state of mind, I also tried a pull at the hookah; for all its aromatic second-hand smoke, the tobacco was so harsh that it felt as if sandpaper had been rubbed inside my throat. It made cigarettes seem like candy sticks.

I finally said good night to Mohsin Khan and crawled into my little tent and my sleeping bag and retired for the night.

The soundtrack to my dream was a magpie robin's song, which I realised a few moments after I awoke. The picture in my head faded away as my sleepiness dissipated; the song played on—a hauntingly wonderful whistle that rose and fell as it followed a natural rhythm. As I opened my tent's flap and ventured outside, my impression was that of awakening from a dream simply to step into another one.

The sun was just creeping over the snow-capped Himalayas and its feeble golden yellow rays were bouncing off the Lidder river to give Pahalgam a golden, warm, honey-like glow. It was to this wonderful colour of dawn that the magpie was singing an ode.

Old Mohsin Khan on the right bank was frantically

gesturing to me. He wanted me to come over to his side. By the time I had gingerly crossed over the makeshift bridge comprising two tree trunks casually thrown across the breadth of the river, he had steaming hot tea ready.

Though most visitors confine themselves to the left bank of the Lidder in Pahalgam, the other bank has fabulous walks amongst the dense woods there. Aru, eleven kilometres away, is a stunningly beautiful place.

Mohsin Khan became my companion for the three days I spent in Pahalgam, and I was very fortunate to have him along. He took me for walks and showed me places I would never have found in any guidebook nor discovered on my own. And one of his grandchildren was always available to guard my tent and my bike while we were away exploring.

When I awoke on the morning of the day I was to leave, the opposite bank was empty; the Khan and his clan had moved on in search of more grazing pastures.

My memory of Pahalgam is automatically twinned with that of the old Khan. I've been to Pahalgam once after that and tried looking for him, but he was nowhere to be found. I asked the butcher and the baker, but they simply shrugged their shoulders and said that the clan doesn't follow any fixed path or plan. I think of him often and wonder whether he bites his tongue or hiccups as he stands in a lofty green pasture grazing his herd.

Down the Barrel of a Gun

*I*started my ride back from Pahalgam to Jammu,
where I planned to load my bike into the Jammu-
Tavi Express to Mumbai and then fly from Jammu to
Delhi and then Mumbai.

My ride started off normally enough. There was
plenty of traffic that consisted of private cars, trucks,
buses and a large number of military vehicles, especially
the handsome, rugged olive green Stallion trucks that
the Indian army uses. At times I was told by the alert
soldiers sitting in the rear of the truck not to overtake
and keep in the middle of the convoy of trucks. But

this was only till the Jawahar Tunnel. After that the going was quite relaxed. At times I would pass road barriers that were open and wave out to the jawans standing guard and they would cheerily wave back and flag me on.

Everyone in Srinagar who knew I was going to ride to Jammu had one common suggestion: stop at Peeda near Ramban and have the rajma-rice there. So I did, although I'm not a big rajma-rice fan. The amount of ghee that was loaded in that dish could have lit up a nineteenth-century palace for a week, but it really was delicious.

After my meal, I kicked the bike to life and swung a leg over the saddle for the last 150 kilometres of my ride. Forty minutes into it, I saw a J&K police van parked across the road with about five policemen standing with their rifles cocked and ready. The inspector leading them was a lad of about twenty-six, whose uniform seemed to be spray painted on him— it fit so snugly over his bulging muscles. But all that was not of consequence to me; what was causing me mild consternation was that he was brandishing his magazine-fed pistol about as he directed his men to get into ambush position. Mild consternation turned into positive panic when I found the nozzle of the gun pointing towards me, and for the second time in five days, I saw a finger curl around a trigger. I was ordered off my Bullet as I rode up to them and roughly hauled towards the inspector.

'Why haven't you been stopping at barriers when you were signalled to do so?' the inspector demanded. I explained that no one had signalled me to stop; in fact, I pointed out, I'd waved to the sentries at all the barriers and they had cheerily flagged me on.

That seemed to anger him even more; he wouldn't take his finger off the trigger, and honestly that wasn't doing a lot of good to my bladder. He called a few of the barrier check-points on his wireless and after some animated conversation came back to me with his fair face even redder with rage.

'Where are your two other companions?' he shouted. When I told him that I'd been riding solo since Leh, he grabbed the lapels of my jacket and through clenched teeth muttered, 'You better start telling the truth or I am going to have you taken to the police station where it will be beaten out of you.'

I repeated once again that I was a travel writer and I could show him my credentials if he would consider for a moment that I was telling the truth instead of just trying to bludgeon me into agreeing that I was lying.

A police van came roaring up to us then, and screeched to a halt just like in the movies. Another inspector got out with a few more constables—more guns and carbines. I'd seen more guns in the last few minutes than I had in all my life. Inspector 2 seemed a reasonable chap: he greeted me with a warm smile and then gently asked if there was anything I wanted to confess. I once again earnestly explained that I had not jumped any barriers or police controls (not after the Zoji La at least), that I was travelling alone and, I confessed after a significant pause, that I really needed to go, raising my little finger just to make sure they understood what I meant. He sent me to the bushes with an armed escort who stood on alert while I went about my business.

Inspector 2 seemed to believe that there was a small possibility that I might be telling the truth. He got onto the wireless and asked the jawans manning the last barrier, which I had supposedly skipped, what time I and my supposed two riding mates had gone through. Once he had the time, he figured that I would have had to have ridden at an average speed of 80kmph to get from there to here in such a short time. I assured him that I couldn't have—not on such a busy road with such a heavily-loaded bike.

Inspector 1 uncurled his finger from around the trigger and holstered his gun, and I started breathing a little easy. As if on cue, three motorcyclists appeared from around the bend in the road. Inspector 1 hurriedly un-holstered his weapon once again and went into attack mode with his bunch of constables. This time they had got the right guys. They were three foreign tourists riding hired Enfield Bullets: one of them was shirtless, another was shoeless, and all three seemed clueless about the consternation they had caused by jumping barriers. They rode towards the policemen exuberantly calling out, 'Juley, juley'—Ladakh's happy word for hello—not realising that Ladakh was a few hundred kilometres behind and a very sticky situation lay ahead.

The two inspectors stopped them, ordered their collective constabulary to guard them, and then walked up to me. They were profusely apologetic; Inspector 1 was now inviting me to the police station for tea and pakoras instead of threats and pastings. Now that the guns and rifles were pointing elsewhere, I decided that I could get a little indignant about the whole thing. Not too much though, because Inspector 1's holster flap was still unbuttoned. I ventured a question about how the radioing barrier police could have confused those sell-them-off-as-scrap motorcycles with mine. No doubt, mine was mud-caked and dusty, but it still looked like Lawrence of Arabia after the great desert crossing; the other bikes looked like beggared Bedouin bandits. He replied that what had been radioed ahead was 'three riders, unshaved, helmets, luggage and thump-thump bikes'.

I could not fault that. I had serious stubble, luggage,

and my bike did have a pronounced thump—more than other Bullets, thanks to its sawed-off 'rocket' silencer. Inspector 2 then gave me a warm hug and wished me all the best for the rest of my ride.

As I rode off, I saw both of them in my rear-view mirror walking towards the three bikers, faces grim and guns in hand . . .

Automotive Love

*I*t's been eight years since that Ladakh, Jammu and Kashmir ride, and I still have the Bullet, although it's now largely used as a mode of lazy transport— meaning I use it for distances that I could and should walk, but am too lazy to. The Bullet is not without its moods, and when I have neglected it too long it shows its displeasure by refusing to start or by suddenly sputtering and stalling during those rare occasions when we are a considerable distance from home.

There is a dent on the top of its fuel tank just below the fuel cap, and almost everyone who runs an eye over my bike notices it. I often get asked about it. Once even a policeman managing traffic saw it and asked me about it. This is because the dent's in a very strange place. I'm evasive when asked though, because I'm quite ashamed of the truth behind the dent. I usually fob off any query by saying that I'd parked the motorcycle under a coconut tree and a ripe coconut landed on the petrol tank, causing the dent.

In truth, this is how it was caused.

It was a hot summer's day and one of those rare times when I'd forsaken the air-conditioned comfort of a car for the quick convenience of my bike. I had things to do in various parts of the city and one day to finish them in. Traffic and parking space made the bike the best option to use that day. Suddenly, half way through my chores, when the sun was at its zenith and perspiration was flowing down me like a river in flood, my Bullet decided to have one of its mood swings. It sputtered a bit and then was fine. I felt a twinge of apprehension in the pit of my belly and then, sure enough, the second sputter followed from which it recovered with a magnificently loud backfire—loud enough to launch the crows from the trees overhead into flight. Then it died. I shifted down two gears into the second and let in the clutch hoping that the plug would spark, the air fuel mixture would combust and the exhaust would roar again. Just like it had at that critical moment outside the hotel in Kargil. But all that came through the exhaust was the low beat of an engine that was being turned by the crank, rather than turning the crank. An engine that was truly dead and sounding like a mournful trumpet at a funeral march.

I rolled to a stop at the side of the road, remained standing astride the bike and tried kick-starting it with my right leg which was soon aching with the effort. I hauled the bike on its stand and tried with my left leg, which too was soon aching after a hundred kicks that didn't as much as bring a sputter of life. It was a busy street choked with exhaust fumes and dust and the temperature was hovering in the very high thirties. I had things to do and here I was stuck with a bike that had run fine for the last four months, had come alive on half a kick this morning, but was now stubbornly refusing to start. For a brief moment I lost my temper, bunched up my fist, and slammed it into the tank.

That is the truth behind the dent.

When I look at it now, I regret that moment of rage, that moment of ingratitude. Yes, my Bullet had packed up at a most inconvenient time, but I was in Mumbai city. I could catch a cab, call a mechanic and get it sorted out. I feel bad that, for a brief moment, I let myself forget that when my life depended on it on hazardous roads that touched the clouds, my Bullet delivered with pluck.

On the bright side, the dent serves as a nice cup holder, and the base of a standard roadside tea glass sits snugly in it whenever I stop to have tea.

The first car I ever drove was my family's 1954 Dodge Kingsway. I learnt clutch control on it, and because I used to drive it round and round my apartment block, I honed my skills at manoeuvring a car through narrow alleys and around tight corners. This was in my very early teens, and the car was gone before I came of age to drive legally.

My first real car after I got my licence to drive was the Maruti Van, a 1985 model with most of its parts imported directly from Japan.

I like to think that if that car could tell its tale, here is what it would say.

My kind arrived in India in the early 1980s and, I can unashamedly say, gave this land's motoring scene a fresh new face. This land where the Premier Padmini was king and the Ambassador was a car whose name was its saving grace. Indians took to my kind because it was a refreshing change, rather than the fact that we were a better breed than the above mentioned. That we were better has been proved over the years, and I look back at my time with a sense of nostalgia as I wait to be repaired so that I can go back home to the gentleman who owns me.

I belong to the old school—proof of which is etched across my engine block in bold letters that spell 'SUZUKI', and parts of me were manufactured in factories in the land of the rising sun. My owner, a man named Saam, bought me on 18 October 1985 when he arrived at the showroom with his wife, his daughter and his son in an old Dodge Kingsway that had seen many a mile in India and was due for retirement. I braced myself as Saam switched on my ignition and fired up my engine for the first time, expecting him to stall at first attempt and strain my clutch because he was used to the big American six-cylinder whose clutch was worn with age and not that sharp anymore. My clutch, on the other hand, was razor sharp and coming off it too hard would either stall me or cause me to shoot ahead with generous wheel spin. But it was my first taste of the man's gentle way of driving—he started me off as smooth as silk without even a hint of a jerk or a lurch. Over the years in which numerous people have occupied the driver's seat, I still heave a sigh of relief when Saam's at the wheel.

I became the premier mode of transport for the family, which welcomed me by garlanding me and breaking eggs and coconuts in front of me. The first five years were relaxed and easy-going; either Saam or his wife drove me and the kids were confined to the rear seat. Once in a while the son would clamour about wanting to drive but a stern word would quell it. Quell it, for the moment, mind you, because the son was a wily one at his game and in his mind the right to drive was a god-given one rather than a privilege. I know for a fact that he once sneaked out the old Dodge Kingsway which the family still owned. The parents were driving me back from a late-night movie and I saw the old Dodge flash past me at Marine Drive, taking cover in the shadow of a bus so that the parents wouldn't see it. But I caught a glimpse of the son crouching behind the wheel, his face white with the fear of being found out.

The prime of my life began when the son came of age to drive. Very rarely in those years when the son was at the wheel did I ever start off without squealing my tyres and burning some rubber. My speedy days began when I, appropriately equipped with a three-trumpet air horn, was four years old and the son eighteen. The law gave him the right to drive but the parents weren't quite convinced yet, and so both of us called in the best problem-solving tactic, namely 'everything's quite all right as long as we're not found out'. The son and his friends would gather at Chetan's vacant apartment under the pretence of studies and then sneak me out in the middle of the night and paint the town red. They would blast loud music and corner me so hard that it put my suspension to the ultimate test and make my engine scream at the red line in every gear.

I enjoyed every moment of it: my 800cc engine was tuned for peak performance, my clutch was razor sharp and my brakes gave inertia a run for its money. What I didn't approve of was their going behind some unsuspecting victim and blasting the horn like a banshee in pain. They made a poor cyclist fall off his cycle in fright once and I felt very bad for the poor guy, so I decided to teach them a lesson.

A few days later I jammed the air horn right behind a cop who was enjoying his tea break at a roadside tea shop. The shock of the high decibel blast made him jump out of his skin and spill all his tea over the front of his spotless white shirt. Poor Rishad was cowering behind the steering wheel, his hair standing at end from what must follow. He'd frantically turned off the ignition, flipped the toggle switch that diverted current to the standard horn, but I hadn't relented. I kept the air horn jammed for twelve seconds. By the end of it a small crowd had gathered around us. The cop was in a thunderous rage and had a few choice swear words to dish out. He made Rishad fork out Rs 200 as a fine and an additional Rs 100 as laundry charges for his shirt. Big money when you have a monthly allowance of Rs 900.

Now, the decades of fast living have taken its toll. I have developed numerous squeaks and rattles; the corrosive Mumbai weather has eaten away at my insides and I suffered a major seizure just as I completed 100,000 kilometres on the clock. My fuel efficiency— which had returned a phenomenal 16kmpl once—has dropped under 10kmpl and my powerplant, which the son or the daughter used to push to 110kmph on a regular night out, can barely make it to 80kmph today. Sometimes the son tries—squeezing bhp from every gear—but I balk and shudder and try to get across to him that I am no spring chicken anymore. Let us resign to the fact that my fast days are past!

We (the son and I) have had scraps with other cars, the building gates and most recently, with a human being. The first has left me scarred and dented and the last shattered my windshield. I wait here now in Pune, to get back to my hometown and my new friend, a brand new Daewoo Matiz. Oh, to be ten years younger . . .

MFA 5381

The Guides

Uncle 'Moustachioed Mukesh'

After the incident with the policemen in Jammu &
Kashmir, I made it a point to give sentries a lot of
leeway at all barriers on my trips thereafter. Anything
that seemed even remotely a gesture to stop—from
swatting a fly to stretching their arms to scratching
their butt—and I would promptly stand on the brakes
and come to a screeching halt. Which is why I'd
stopped at the border between Gujarat and Rajasthan
on my way to Jaisalmer.

I was taking the back road into Jaisalmer, driving up from Ahmedabad via Mehsana, Deesa and Barmer. The splendid, arrow-straight road built through the desert is called NH 15. Because of its proximity to the border, the road sees very little traffic—tourists heading to Jaisalmer use the busier highways via Jodhpur or Jaipur. It's a shame, really. The 550-odd kilometre road from Ahmedabad goes through a part of Rajasthan that isn't preening for the foreign tourist.

The sentry at the Gujarat-Rajasthan border was quite surprised when I screeched to a halt—he had probably been cheerily waving me on—but quickly recovered to start acting important. He asked me where I had come from and where I was headed to and brought out a register for me to fill. The entry of the last date on it was in the late 1980s.

I've often noticed that these chaps at lonely barrier postings like this one somehow seem to have an affinity for making conversation. Soon, Gagan Chandra from Gorakhpur was asking me about Mumbai and Bollywood. He signalled to a man in the small tea stall on the opposite side of the road for two cups of tea. And at the very indication that tea would be coming, an ascetic seemed to materialise. I realised he had been sitting on his haunches partly hidden by the wall of the barrier post. He was dressed in the saffron of sadhus, ash was smeared across his forehead and his gray hair and beard grew like wild weed in an untended garden. He signalled the chai walla manning the stove too, and he did it so fervently that I thought he was trying to invoke a cup of tea from the heavens above. The chai walla, though, returned a careless gesture indicating that the sadhu would be getting nothing. Gagan Chandra explained that he was the local sadhu, at the same time pointing to his forehead with his index finger and twirling it about. In case I didn't understand that gesture, he added that most locals believed the man was a little 'off the rails'. Whenever someone from the barrier post asked for tea, he would demand a cup. Sometimes the owner of the tea stall felt sorry for him and gave him tea, but he didn't seem to be in a generous mood that day.

I gestured to the tea man that I would pay for the sadhu's tea, and when the cups arrived, the sadhu walked up to me and said, 'Thank you very much, Sir, for your kindness and this cup of tea.' In the Queen's English. In an accent that was spot-on British. Give an eager barber half an hour with this man and replace his saffron dhoti and kurta with a suit from Savile Row, and he could pass off as an affluent British gent of Indian origin at Pall Mall. He seemed to enjoy the look of astonishment on my face, because his eyes were twinkling with merriment.

'You're wondering about my accent, aren't you?' he

smiled. I nodded. He explained that as a young lad he'd studied in a school in south India that was run by English missionaries, then gone to university in Durham, England for further education, after which he'd worked there for a while.

So how did he come to be here on this dusty road depending on a chai walla's magnanimity for a cup of tea?

'Karma,' he shrugged, and that was that.

But it was he who told me the following story about the creation of the Thar desert, where Jaisalmer stands.

Years ago, farther back than where you can cast your mind, Lord Ram stood at the tip of the great Indian peninsular, poised to launch the invasion on the isle of Lanka. He was doing this to do away with Ravana who had been a naughty sort of chap and run off with Ram's wife, Sita.

The engineers from Ram's army of motivated monkeys and brawny bears had laid the plans for the bridge across the sea and construction was about to start when the God of the Sea erupted from the depths of the Palk Straits. Dripping wet (obviously) and angry, he announced that he wouldn't allow the bridge to be built across his domain.

Ram gave his 'I'm a man of peace' smile and tried to justify his Lankan campaign, but the Sea God wouldn't relent. It was the deafening twang of a bowstring as Ram let fly a heavenly arrow that jerked the oceanic lord into the realisation that this God knew more than just how to smile, so he promptly apologised. Ram immediately sent up a prayer to the weapons controller sitting somewhere amongst the clouds in the heavens above and asked for the direction of the arrow to be changed.

The arrow then turned around from its southerly direction and headed northwest where it crash-landed, rendering the entire region an arid desert.

The place where the arrow landed is near modern-day Jaisalmer, and this is the legend about the creation of the Thar desert.

It had been an entertaining tea break with the sentry and the sadhu, but I had to be on my way since I had quite a long road yet ahead. NH 15 goes through Sanchor, Barmer and Devikot, all dusty desert towns. The low shrub bordering the road affords superb visibility and this allows reasonably high speeds. The speedometer needle on the Maruti Baleno I was driving often nudged 170kmph, but it wasn't a good idea to go so fast, as I realised when I stopped at Barmer to stretch my legs. I had hit a crow who hadn't been able to fly out of my path fast enough and the impact had smashed the number plate. Beyond Barmer there were more peacocks in the air than crows and I kept the speed down. Hitting a peacock at 170kmph could wipe out the peacock, the car and me.

There was no way of not knowing I was getting close to Jaisalmer since hoardings and hotel advertisements started appearing a few kilometres before I reached the city. This might indicate that Jaisalmer is yet another Rajasthan tourist hotspot, but when I saw the ancient and proud fort rising like an apparition, the rays of the setting sun imparting a burnt honey colour to the sandstone, I realised this fort couldn't be dismissed as a mere 'tourist attraction'. Apart from its beauty and grandeur, it's a symbol of the hardy survival instincts that characterised the kings and people of Rajputana.

Founded by the Bhatti Rajput ruler around 1156 AD, the fort was strategically placed on the old caravan route between Delhi and Central Asia. The rise of the shipping trade and the port of Mumbai saw the caravans slowing down to a trickle and then Partition sealed off the ancient trade route.

The town would have gone the Hampi way and become a ruin if it were not a perfect border outpost as was proved in the 1971 Indo-Pak war. Obviously tourism has discovered it. It has all the ingredients of a mystical Indian destination. An old and proud fort with a maze of colourful bazaars within, desert for miles around that's perfect for camel safaris, loads of history . . . the tourists come like bees to honey.

I settled into my hotel on the Sam Sand Dunes Road and then asked the chap at the reception where I could take a few good pictures to capture the essence of Jaisalmer. He suggested I hire a guide and he knew just the right person—his uncle.

I decided to let this obvious attempt to enhance family income pass. I needed someone who knew the city well, and if his uncle knew his way around, then there was no harm in hiring his services.

Uncle, who arrived at the dot of 5.30 the next morning, was a local schoolteacher with a large moustache and a healthy belly. He considered himself the singer Mukesh's biggest fan. If there ever was more than a minute's lapse of communication between us, he'd give his whiskers a whimsical stroke and start whispering the lyrics of a Mukesh song from a Raj Kapoor flick. A whisper that would soon reach a crescendo sung with enough passion to make both Raj Kapoor and Mukesh roll in their graves. He, of course, thought his voice was as smooth as silk and could carry the same strain of sorrow that Mukesh was so good at—when in fact it had the abrasiveness of heavy-duty factory grade sandpaper.

The first place he led me to was a point a few kilometres away from the fort, where he told me to stand and just look at the edifice. The entire fort seemed to come alive as the first rays of the sun from the east hesitantly shimmered on the surface of the walls, and then rapidly strengthened in intensity. The fort must have gone through a thousand shades from the dark gray it was before the sun came up, to the bright amber it finally turned to in a matter of three minutes.

That done, we headed towards the havelis. The intricate carvings, magnificent design and the sheer richness that these homes exude are an indication of how prosperous the people here were once upon a time. The Patwon ki Haveli was originally built between 1800 and 1860 by five Jain brothers. Today two of the six segments house their descendants, two contain craft shops and two are owned by the Archaeological Survey of India. My Mukesh reincarnate explained that for the residents, the haveli is like a golden cage. The government refuses to let them sell it to any individual or company, nor are they willing to buy it. If the family leaves, the government will move in.

He had another interesting story about the haveli of Salim Singh Mohta, built in the 1600s. This ambitious prime minister tried to rival the Maharaja by building two more storeys to the haveli so it would stand taller than the king's palace. The Maharaja promptly tore the storeys down. I guess the 'mine is bigger than yours' competition between men is as old as time itself.

Standing on top of the haveli and taking in the desert all around, I asked my guide whether people here ever longed for the sight of the sea or some kind of water body. He smirked and asked me to follow him. Three verses of '*Dil jalta hain*' later we reached Gadi Sagar. This sparkling blue artificial lake was created by Maharaja Gadi Singh in 1367 to provide water to the residents. There are numerous chhatris in the middle of the lake where the kings used to repose with their queens, mistresses and whomsoever caught their fancy.

By the time we finally walked into the fort, it was already teeming with tourists; yet I still felt as if I'd stepped back a couple of centuries. (The illusion would have been complete if not for the electric lines that spread like ugly cobwebs across every courtyard and narrow alley.) Jaisalmer fort is a living fort: people reside inside it like they did in the olden days. The seven Jain temples inside are a marvel of architecture too. One particular temple is built for musical performances and is a feat of sorts in acoustic engineering. There happened to be a group of German tourists there and—to my slight embarrassment—my guide decided to give them a splendid demo of the temple's sound-dynamics, cooing away to a voluptuous woman in stone as if she were Nargis in *Barsaat*. It was truly a measure of the temple designer's skill that Uncle managed to sound almost musical.

But despite his distorted harmonics, Uncle was quite knowledgeable about the fort and its surroundings. He pointed out a gate called the Hawa Pol (breeze gate) and, stepping through it, I was greeted with a blast of cold air, a relief from the heat that had started to rise. The stone ledges by the side of the gates were worn to a shine from generations of backsides that must have reposed on them to escape the sweltering summer heat of the fortress.

We'd seen more of the day than the sun itself, and now it was beating down hard. We had some fabulous lassi in one of the small restaurants that crowd the narrow lanes in the fort and headed out for lunch.

The restaurants around the fort do fabulous Rajasthani thalis, truly terrific on the tongue though hard on the stomach, thanks to the spice and oil. The Rajasthani thali is a work of culinary craftsmanship. Each vegetable, curry and snack was so tasty, I simply couldn't decide what to eat and what to forgo. Just the number and variety of pickles would have outnumbered the items on the menu of a fast food chain. While I gave up after the third helping, Uncle ploughed through all that was served, his mouth working like a blacksmith's bellows feeding a furnace. Often he would stop chewing, widen his eyes and draw out the dramatic silence caused by the absence of his high-decibel chomping, put one hand on his belly and the other in the air like a Nazi salute and let out some of the most flagrant belches I have ever heard. It was a hum that started deep in his belly, developed into a rumble as it ran up his gullet and then reached a crescendo in a combination of a moan and a grunt as it blew through his mouth to the world outside. It was as if he were sending the cook a message in belch code, complimenting him on the fine fare.

The next morning I set off on a two-day camel safari. My friend at the hotel reception had told me that a group from the hotel was going on a safari, and that they were looking for a fourth person to share the costs, so I decided to join them. They were three English tourists—a man, his wife and sister-in-law.

They were two days very well spent. I was taken aback at how populated the seemingly desolate desert is. There are little villages all over, where life has been going on for centuries. The Rajasthan government has dug bore wells in every village and the hand pump over these wells stands in the centre of each village. Every well we passed seemed so colourful because of the brightly-dressed women gathered around. After the monotonous dun hue of the desert, the splash of colour the womenfolk offered would always be a soothing balm to the eyes.

My newfound friends were often moved to tears when they saw grubby children running about, womenfolk carrying water back to their houses and yet others collecting dung and drying it to use as fuel for their cooking fires. I tried to explain to them that these villagers were probably happier and more content with their lives than most urbanites are. They have everything that they need to exist, they count their wealth in terms of the number of healthy cattle and livestock that they have, and their farming gives them food for their bellies. Their thatched mud huts give them adequate shelter from the elements. This is the life they have known for generations and are satisfied with it.

At night, we'd sit around the campfire and listen to the camel riders' tales about the valour of the Rajputs. Tales that were evidently straight from the horse's mouth: one camel rider claimed to be the direct descendent of Rana Pratap, while another went further, stating that he believed he was the Rana reincarnated.

These extravagant stories were fuelled by the liquid refreshment that they were always able to find in the villages near which we stopped for the night. My co-campers were well read and good company; we had many interesting conversations after dinner and they lasted long after the campfire had burned down to smoking embers.

These are pleasant memories of that safari and they help me forget less desirable ones of backside aches and chaffed thighs. I also wish I could retain the tan I acquired from the hot desert sun, but that has faded away. The era of Rajputs and fierce battles has faded away too, but the Jaisalmer fort and the atmosphere it creates of a time long gone lives on. It will be many, many years before this fort crumbles and fades into oblivion.

S.N. Keshav Murthy

Like the fort at Jaisalmer, I consider any ancient monument a time cell, a little module that has frozen an era within its walls for eternity. Life may go on at a frenzied pace all around its periphery, but within its ramparts or its carved walls, history looks you in the face as you stare at a legacy of talent, art and architectural science left behind from centuries ago. In other words, I'm fond of visiting temples and archaeological sites.

Temples in my country make me proud. The magnitude of creativity that they exude is only enhanced by the fact that they were built in times when the most powerful processors of the day were grey cells lodged in a human head. This struck me particularly in Belur, in southern Karnataka. The Chennakesava temple is tucked away in a corner, and if you're just driving through Belur on the way to Chikmagalur, you won't even see it. By the time I had tackled the haphazard traffic, turned left at the Y junction and passed the bus stand, I'd almost given up any hopes of finding one of Karnataka's most famous temples. And then there it was. The seven-storey gopuram that marks the entrance is the one that was rebuilt after fourteenth-century raiders charged down this very road to destroy and pillage it.

The entire complex stands on a raised platform along which visitors can park their cars. As soon as I got out of my car I was charged at by nine locals yelling 'buy please, buy please'; one wanted to sell me 'authentic' coins that he claimed to have excavated himself, five others were pushing pictorial guides right in my face, so close that I could smell the ink and paper. Number seven and eight were selling roasted groundnuts. The last one had nothing to sell but since he was loitering around with no particular plan of action, he probably thought he'd get his daily lesson on how to hassle a tourist.

After kindly, smilingly, assertively, firmly and finally angrily refusing their wares and failing to convince them, I engaged my standard 'tout/hawker repellent'. I made a ring with my thumb and forefinger, put it into my mouth against my folded tongue and let out the loudest, most piercing whistle to ever ring through Belur.

The 'buy please' bandwagon, right at the epicentre of this high frequency blast, scattered as if Hiroshima had happened amidst them, clutching their ears in agony. After that no one came within ten feet of me. My high-pitched restraining order had worked again. Well, almost . . .

S.N. Keshav Murthy came up to me dressed in a black coat cut to a style that was in vogue when the Indian National Congress used to gather in Azad Maidan during the Quit India movement. He politely handed me his card as if we were meeting at a cocktail function. He informed me, in perfect unaccented English, that he had observed my tactics and that they wouldn't work with him. He told me that he was hard of hearing anyway, and to him my piercing whistle had sounded as sweet as the flute that represents the bird in Prokofiev's *Peter and the Wolf*.

There was something about his neatly combed white hair, gentle manner and the fact that he had a passion for Western classical music that warmed me to this elderly man. I read his card; it told me that he was a government-recognised guide, and I at once hired his services.

This was in 2004, and the manner in which Mr Murthy took me around the Chennakesava temple gave me an education that has helped me understand temples and sculptures ever since. He didn't, like most guides, talk in a monotone, as if he were disgorging a story told a thousand times. He took me around, showed me sculptures and, instead of just telling me what they were meant to depict, asked for my views, told me to apply logic, recall mythology, and put all my inferences together as if completing a jigsaw puzzle. The going was slow at first, but as soon as I got the hang of it, it became great fun. I remember those sculptures and what they mean to this day.

The temple at Belur is around nine hundred years old. It is believed to have been consecrated in 1117 AD. Started by Vishnuvardhana, the Hoysala king, it was finally completed by his grandson 103 years later.

The walls of the temple are adorned with dancing figures and Mr Murthy asked me to look carefully at them. I realised that each and every figure (forty-two of them) was the same voluptuous woman. It was astonishing to me that—even after so many centuries— the features had stood the test, and were detailed enough to make it apparent that it was the same woman, depicted in different poses. The woman, incidentally, was Vishnuvardhana's queen Shantala Devi, renowned for her beauty.

As we walked across the paved compound, Mr Murthy explained that the temple was not just built for ornamental purposes. Each of the 15,000 carvings had some meaning. In those days, temples were multipurpose: they served as places of worship as well as for education. To elucidate this, he took me over to a carving showing a boy of about sixteen looking adoringly at a woman with the head of a donkey. Mr Murthy explained that this was a way to tell adolescent boys that, at sixteen, when your hormones are working overtime and flowing out of your ears, even a donkey looks hot ... so learn to differentiate between love and lust!

We'd started from the rear of the temple as there was a lot of crowd up front and now, as they dispersed, we made our way to the front. The entrance is guarded by fierce monsters in stone and beside them is the royal emblem of the Hoysalas—the young Sala killing a lion.

The story behind this emblem goes that when the young king Sala was attending his gurukul, a lion suddenly appeared, and while the other students ran away in fear, Sala stood up to the lion's charge. His teacher shouted, 'Hoy! Sala', meaning, 'Kill it, Sala', hence the name Hoysala.

To point out sculptures higher up on the walls, Mr Murthy fished out a tiny mirror and used the sun's reflection to highlight the sculpture he was referring to. The most astounding fact of some of the sculptures higher up on the walls is that they are freestanding bracket figures, which are angled between the upper walls and the overhanging eaves. It must have taken a lot of skill to carve them with the tools of the day and the fact that they are standing today speaks volumes of the workmanship.

Though he was registered as a guide at the Belur temple, I was so impressed with Mr Murthy that I requested him to come with me to Halebid and show me around the Hoysaleshwara temple there. He readily agreed and as we were driving the scenic 18 kilometres between the two temples, he filled me up on the history of Halebid.

This town, which was the centre of commerce and the capital of the Hoysala empire at the beginning of the twelfth century, was called Dorasamudra, a name that referred to the huge artificial lake to the east of the city. Famed for its wealth and culture, it got its share of unwanted attention like all prosperous cities of those times, and was attacked and ransacked by the Sultans of Delhi during the early part of the fourteenth century. But its period of prosperity spawned frenetic building activity. The city was abandoned after the Hoysala empire came to an end with the last king, Ballala the Third, dying in battle in 1342.

We reached the temple just as he finished his narrative and the Hoysaleshwara temple came into view. Standing amidst green lawns, the entrance to the complex is from the north but the temple stands facing the east, looking over that ancient artificial lake that gave the old capital its name.

The temple is, of course, regal. Halebid, or Halebeedu, means 'old town', to distinguish it from the developments after it was ransacked. But the temple still stands tall like a symphony in stone, an unfinished symphony rather, because construction was never finished. As a matter of fact, there are blank sections on the walls where sculptors meant to work their magic but were interrupted by the invading hordes.

Impressive are the two huge monolithic statues of Nandi and the breathtaking details on the doors of the sanctum. To make me understand the magnitude of labour that went into creating these stone masterpieces, Mr Murthy took me into the temple and showed me the huge round stone pillars that supported the carved roof. Each pillar was lathe-turned to circular perfection. Imagine turning a one-ton rock on a manually-operated lathe!

So engrossed was I by Mr Murthy's conversation and stories and the temples themselves, that at both Belur and Halebid I didn't take a single picture. Recently, when I was passing by on my way to Chikmagalur, I stopped at Belur to look him up and take a few pictures. I was told by one of the other guides that Mr Murthy had passed away a few months back. Mr Murthy may have been a simple temple guide, but he got his daughters through school and college and I remember him telling me that all three of them were now settled in the US.

Ashutosh Tripathi

During my last two years as a travel correspondent for an auto magazine, I was dating a pretty photographer originally from Chandigarh but working in Mumbai. For the purpose of this narrative I shall call her Amanda. She shared my enthusiasm for travel and very often I would buy her a flight ticket so she could fly out to the nearest airport where I would be waiting. She would breeze out of the airport and hop into the car laughing with delight that she'd made the flight because Amanda and time didn't really see eye to eye. Her grouse with it was that it always moved at the same pace except when she was asleep—she was sure it picked up speed then and rushed towards morning, because however much she slept, it was never enough.

On one such occasion I'd driven from Delhi via Agra and Gwalior and was now waiting for her at the Khajuraho airport. Amanda had flown from Mumbai to Delhi the previous night and was now on a flight to this town famous for its erotic sculptures. The flight—which goes from Delhi to Khajuraho via Varanasi—is invariably late. Also, it was winter, a time when Delhi is shrouded in fog causing delays in take-off and landings.

Though I had been to Khajuraho before, I'd never seen its airport; I've always driven to the little town from Delhi. It reminded me of those little village train stations—quaint and charming. I headed to the canteen, where I sat under the shade and sipped on chai, waiting for the flight to land. A bunch of guides were waiting outside the Arrivals gate to offer their services to tourists. One of them came and sat down next to me, a glass of tea in his hand. He had a guide's badge clipped to his shirt and he told me he was waiting for his clients to arrive. We got talking and Ashutosh Tripathi turned out to be a history graduate from the University of Gwalior. From the conversation I realised that, like S.N. Keshava Murthy, he too wasn't someone who'd simply memorised the history of Khajuraho to narrate to his clients. His knowledge about the place came from a deep-rooted fondness for this little village and respect for those who created it.

'The flight is always overbooked, because for tourists with little time, flying here is the best option,' he told me.

Indeed I knew this well, because even in today's well-connected India, Khajuraho is a fifteen-hour drive from Delhi. A round trip from Delhi to Khajuraho and back is just 150 kilometres short of driving from Mumbai to Delhi. Despite the pressures of population in the country, and practically every square kilometre being developed, Khajuraho still retains that feeling of being in the middle of nowhere.

The lure of peeking into the sexual trends of ancient India is so great that temples that were built a thousand years ago, during the ninth and tenth centuries, today sustain the economy of a little village deep in the heart of India.

But it is its location that could have been Khajuraho's saviour, Ashutosh told me. He narrated the following story that he'd heard from a village elder who had heard it from his grand uncle who had read it somewhere.

Al-Sultan al-Azam wal Khaqan al-Mukarram Abdul Muzaffar Muhiuddin Muhammad Aurangzeb Bahadur Alamgir I Padshah Ghazi took a deep sigh of resignation and turned his attention to the chief of internal espionage. (I interrupted Ashutosh here to say that it was a bloody good thing Aurangzeb, with the might of the Mughal army behind him, could walk into any dominion that caught his fancy. Imagine trying to fill up an immigration form with a name like that.)

The wiry man was wrapped in a shawl that also covered his face; a tiny opening allowed his eyes to shine through. The nature of his job demanded he often go incognito. Aurangzeb himself didn't really know what the man looked like, but he'd come to recognise and read the eyes. From the spy's gaze he could tell whether the news was good or bad. He drew a weary breath once again and braced himself for bad news. His master spy always had bad news these days, what with the Marathas constantly rampaging across the border into his Deccan empire and Mewar growing stronger by the day. Plus he had a nagging worry that a threat was forming on his western seaboard. The redcoats, who had arrived barely a century ago as traders, had built up a formidable array of battleships and fortified their factories. One of the captains of his navy had seen one of their menacing-looking battleships fire a ball and could hardly believe that a cannon ball could be shot so far. A gut feeling told Aurangzeb that these merchants of silks and spices had military designs on Hindustan.

But it wasn't anything to do with threats to his rule that the spy had to report. In fact his eyes sparkled and his forehead flushed with a touch of colour as he narrated what he'd stumbled upon during his mission to Bengal. As he spoke, of a group of temples overgrown by the jungle and forgotten by all, 152 kos southeast of Delhi, even Aurangzeb's ears turned red. He couldn't believe that graphic depictions of scenes that were even out of place behind the silk curtains of his perfumed harem, were boldly displayed for all to see. He would not tolerate such brazenness within the boundaries of his realm. He summoned the captain of one of his rapid action units. These units were the elite of the Mughal cavalry and could mobilise at very short notice. He ordered the spy master to lead the captain and his unit on a 'seek and demolish' mission to the group of temples. But a spy, incognito or not, has many enemies, and as it turned out he was found the next morning in a questionable part of Delhi with a dagger buried to the hilt in his back.

And with him died the location of Khajuraho, and that saved the town and its temples.

Just as he finished this very interesting story, the monochrome TV screen outside the Arrivals gate flashed a further delay to Amanda's flight. I ordered more cups of tea and asked Ashutosh to tell me more about the lesser-known facts of Khajuraho.

He told me that the eternal female of Khajuraho who demands—and receives—constant adulation from a steady stream of tourists, domestic and international, conforms to an eye-pleasing 36-24-34. She is rendered magnificently on stone, be it as an apsara, a dancing girl or a nymph. She has a voluptuousness that will never go out of style. This is true because I have often stared at her and have realised that she is curvy, not corpulent; her figure is full but not fleshy.

I asked Ashutosh if she was created from the salacious imagination of those ancient sculptors or if they had models posing for them. Ashutosh shrugged and said that it's one of those facts that will forever remain shrouded in mystery.

I then asked him, 'Why so much sex? I've seen erotica on the walls of the Sun temple in Konark, Vithala temple in Hampi, Bhoramdeo temple in Chhattisgarh and also at the Hoysala temple in Halebid. But, in these places, the erotica needs to be sought out with the help of a guide. But here you can't hide from it! Poses and positions, techniques and tricks, combinations and convolutions ... one blissfully smiling gentleman even demonstrates how a donkey can be used for more than just riding. I mean, it's surprising why the Archaeological Survey of India hasn't put up a sign saying, "Try this at your own risk"!'

I was referring to the Lakshmana temple which usually has tourists wide-eyed with wonder. That evening I saw even Amanda flush a bright shade of pink in front of those friezes.

Ashutosh smiled and explained that there were a few theories. One theory was that these were lessons on stone to show young temple priests the way to marital bliss, as they would have spent their lives cloistered within the temple walls. Another theory is that Indra, the god of thunder, apparently liked watching couples making love, and medieval artisans thought the carvings and sculptures were as good a bribe as any to protect their work from lightning. Well, it seems to have worked—if there was ever a grand capital here, nothing of it remains but the temples.

Ashutosh's last theory is one I like to believe. 'Khajuraho's erotic art simply celebrates the joy of procreation that forms the fundamental rung of any society,' he said seriously. 'That could explain why everyday scenes are woven into the erotica. The sculptors were simply depicting life as they saw it.' It is quite a plausible theory: everybody thinks of sex, everybody enjoys it and those ancient sculptors were simply not coy about it.

Khajuraho was rediscovered by T.S. Burt in 1838. Living in Victorian England, his knowledge of lovemaking till then probably came from a book titled 'The Young English Man's Guide to Sex', which most certainly would have had all of two pages—one titled 'Man on Top', and the other 'Woman on Top'. Ashutosh told me that he was quite sure that Burt must have tugged at his stiff collar to let off some steam and felt his heart hammering in his ears.

With that we finished our fourth cup of tea and the scream of jet engines going into a reverse thrust told us that a plane had touched down. I bid Ashutosh goodbye and thanked him for one of the most entertaining waits I've had at an airport.

And Then There's the Food, Of Course

Balbir Singh's Dhaba, Grand Trunk Road

I've often driven the road from Delhi to Chandigarh and looked for the authentic dhaba experience; rarely have I been able to find it. On one trip, when Chetan and I were driving beyond Ambala on the Grand Trunk Road to Pathankot, we thought there'd be a good chance of finding an authentic dhaba, since we were heading deeper into Punjab. The land of milk and butter, where pinds and parothas are a matter of pride—

surely we would find an authentic dhaba here.

This road has plenty of dhabas, of course. There's usually a large signboard proclaiming the name— Punjab da Dhaba or Shere-e-Punjab Dhaba or some such fanciful moniker. Even more prominent than the name, though, is the Pepsi or the Coca Cola signboard with the smiling visage of some Bollywood or cricketing celebrity. Then there are decorations and lights (largely vast, arrayed banks of tube lights) to give the place a festive air. The menu offers all types of cuisines, making one wonder how people of so many nationalities— including Afghans, Chinese and Keralites—exist harmoniously inside the small and stuffy kitchen. These are the pseudo dhabas—these restaurants with their refrigerators, gas cookers and food processors. The authentic ones rarely ever have flags and lights to attract your attention. And the one sure-shot way you can tell the authenticity of a dhaba is by the trucks parked in front of it, and the neatly laid-out charpois.

We turned into one such place that chilly night— and then looked at each other, wondering whether we should get out of the car or give this place a miss; it looked so drab and run down. There were people sitting cross-legged on charpois and eating. Very close to the charpois was a tank where vessels were being washed and one truck driver was taking a bath dressed in his striped shorts.

We were both extremely hungry though, and finally I think it was the appetising aroma of rotis being pulled out of the red hot tandoor wafting into the car that convinced us.

An elementary school blackboard had 'Balbir Singh's Dhaba' scrawled on it in white chalk. Two zero watt bulbs hanging in the dark interior of the dhaba provided the lighting. The outside was quite well lit by moonlight. All the other clientele consisted of truckers wrapped in their burly shawls to keep out the cold.

As soon as we settled down into a charpoi, a burly sardar came over and handed us a battered jug that had its handle welded in three places. It was full of water meant for washing up. Next to us, a driver and cleaner duo had been handed their jug a few minutes ago and were well into the washing-up process, complete with seven track stereo sound. First deep cleansing gargles to loosen up the gunkiness of the throat. Then came the hawking to expel phlegm, followed by staccato spitting. We tried to emulate the process with as much aural splendour to fit in, but we sounded like a string quartet in the face of a full philharmonic orchestra.

'Can I have a tissue please?' I asked after gargles had been done, and gobs had been spit out. I was reluctantly handed a piece of a week-old newspaper.

The charpois had a narrow wooden plank in the centre across it. This served as our table, and two steel glasses were slammed down on it. Once again, the glasses had very little semblance to their original shape, possibly after years of battling the crushing grips of truck drivers. Mine in fact stood upright only when filled with water.

The menu here existed only in the sardar's mind and he rattled off the dishes available in an accented drawl. There were very many variations of paneer, chicken in various gravies and an array of dals, including the all-time favourite, dal fry.

A huge clay oven with regular openings where vessels could be heated and a cavernous tandoor for parathas dominated the kitchen. Large aluminium vessels containing gravies and pre-cooked pulses and vegetables stood in neat rows. As soon as we'd given our order, Balbir Singh got out a blackened saucepan and started firebombing it with spices and gravies and a multitude of condiments that would each add its unique flavour to our food. Within a few minutes the concoction was emanating a mouth-watering aroma. We moved in for the kill when it was served but were restrained by a sharp yell from Balbir Singh who was lumbering towards us with a bucket.

'Oye! Wait, it's not ready as yet,' he called out. He dipped into the bucket with a small vessel and poured out 100ml of desi ghee into the steaming main dish.

I wanted to yell out cholesterol, cardiac arrest, artery

blockage, obesity!—but I doubted it would make any serious difference. The rotis arrived and in went the cup again to emerge overflowing with clarified butter, this time to be liberally spread over the steaming rotis. I pleaded with the proprietor that fighting the battle of the bulge takes up a major part of my life and this was seriously tilting the scales in the enemy's favour. The man had a simple reasoning: 'If you don't have a big stomach how will the world know you are prosperous, and if you are not prosperous no one will respect you, so shut up and eat!'

Laughter broke out from the other diners in the dhaba, some of them patting their ridiculously large bellies with pride. Fatty and unhealthy as it may sound, the food was heavenly, and I don't say this just because we were ravenous. It was quite simply one very tasty meal.

Once we'd worked our way through the three dishes and a dozen rotis, the owner asked us whether we wanted lassi. I timidly voiced my apprehension about the curd being sour, as there was no refrigerator. A deathly silence descended over the entire dhaba as Balbir Paaji's hair stood on end; in the dim light of the zero watt bulb, his scowling visage looked frightening. He promptly took out two large steel glasses, poured lassi into them—each glass must have taken in at least 400ml of the rich beverage—and put them in front of us. The other customers waited with bated breath for us to take the first sip, and the sardar stood akimbo next to our charpoi. The lassi was, of course, delicious; so delicious that we had seconds. But the proprietor refused to include it in the bill. He explained that we hadn't ordered it, rather he had offered it to protect his reputation (sour curd indeed!) and he couldn't put a price on his reputation.

The satisfying meal brought on some fitful slumber and we crashed out on the charpois itself for the remainder of the night. Next morning, fortified by refreshing tea, we left at dawn.

Whenever I'm on that road, I make it a point to stop by old Balbir's dhaba. It's been nine years since my first meal there, and now Balbir Singh greets me like an old friend. But, to this day, he refuses to include lassi in the bill.

Ahdoos, Lal Chowk, Srinagar

Whenever Shapur and I are out for a meal, we have a standard benchmark against which we judge the quality of food at a restaurant. The benchmark is called the Ahdoos Scale. I've been to very fancy places with liveried waiters and fancy china, simple utilitarian places with lip-smacking food, and places that are a combination of both, but they rarely measure high up on the Ahdoos Scale. Wake up Shapur in the middle of the night and ask him: Your best meal ever?

'Ahdoos.'

We'd driven into Srinagar in a long haul from Chandigarh and had managed to find an unoccupied houseboat on the Dal. I tried to find Riyaz and my old houseboat from a few years ago, but they were gone. So we chose another one, settled in and set off to look for dinner. We'd only snacked on tea and biscuits on the long drive and we were both ravenous now.

If one's a meat eater, there is really no question about being in Srinagar and not going to Ahdoos. I'd been there twice before and each time it had been a delight. Its interiors are quite simple and look as if a half-hearted attempt has been made to create an ambience. We settled down and an eager young Kashmiri lad came up to take the order.

'One gushtaba, one rishtaba.'

'Sir, either have the gushtaba or the rishtaba. Both will be too much.'

Gushtaba and rishtaba are both made with mutton that has been painstakingly pounded into paste and then moulded into golf ball-size pieces. The spices used for each are different, so rishtaba has a red gravy and gushtaba, a pale yellow one. Both are equally tasty.

'No, you get both.'

'Okay . . .'

He started to walk away when we called him back.

'One tabak maaz. No! Make that two tabak maaz.' Tabak maaz is a rack of goat ribs that has been deep fried with all the fat intact. It has a strong meaty flavour, and if you like lamb or mutton, you will agree it's a supremely tasty dish.

'Sir, one will be enough, our portions are very big.'

But we insisted on two. We also insisted on korma and steamed rice, some salad and shahi phirni at the end of it all. The poor lad was scribbling so fast to keep up that his pencil was almost smoking. By this time, going by the mountain of food we had ordered, he was convinced that a large party was going to join us.

The food started arriving and the waiters had to join another table to ours to accommodate the serving dishes. And then they were treated to an exhibition of appreciation for their food like never before. It was so delicious that we polished off every last bit, from the meat to the last onion ring in the salad to the last grain of rice. All that was left were the flat and short ribs of the tabak maaz. In fact, by the time we finished, not only were all the waiters goggle-eyed with wonder, even the old bearded khansama or cook was poking his head from behind the kitchen doors and toothily smiling ear to ear.

'That was an amazing meal,' Shapur exclaimed amidst soft belches.

'Let's knock the cook on the head, bundle him up in the boot and take him back to Mumbai,' I suggested. And we both turned slowly to pointedly stare at the cook with a look not unlike that of wolves eyeing a flock of rotund sheep.

The cook, it seemed, understood a smattering of English. His indulgent smile dissolved into consternation and his head disappeared like a reverse jack-in-the-box. After that he wouldn't even come out when we wanted to congratulate him on the fine meal. He sent a rather shivering sous chef with a tray of kawha tea, the metal cups clattering with his nervousness, to accept our compliments.

When the bill was handed over, we realised that we didn't have enough cash. The proprietor took my credit card and crossed the street to a shop where there was a swiping machine. The shop owner swiped my card there and then paid the proprietor cash. This is not a courtesy they would extend to everyone, he told me afterwards. 'But the justice you have done to our food today is a landmark in this restaurant's history, and it is the least that I can do.'

Chill Thrill

I am a road trip enthusiast, not a race driver. That doesn't mean I don't like speed. I love speed. One of my first happy memories is riding upfront on my dad's 1965 model Vespa and seeing the wavering speedometer needle climb as I felt the wind in my face and hair.

At the beginning of my twenties, my most cherished possession was my Rajdoot Yamaha RD 350. It was fast and unforgiving. Often I would turn a corner too hard, trying to stretch the laws of physics. Sometimes I got away with it, other times friction burns were almost certain. At speeds in excess of 100kmph, its brakes were more like a puppy's lick rather than a Rottweiler's bite. I have scars and memories of crashes associated with it—I loved that bike though.

So, as I said, I like speed. But I don't enjoy being in a race and compelled to drive fast. Being a rally driver would definitely not be the ideal profession for me. However, one of my assignments during my years with *Autocar India* was to go forth and take part in the Raid-de-Himalaya—the world's highest automobile rally.

In rallies, there are always two-man teams. In this one, I was the driver and there was a navigator who would instruct me on the route and tell me what speed I should drive at. I shall call this person Jack.

The Raid-de-Himalaya calls for fast and skilful driving on narrow mountain roads that rarely give second chances; terror and excitement are invisible but constant passengers riding with you. Starting at Shimla, the rally runs through the prettiest parts of Himachal Pradesh and the stark landscapes of Ladakh. The route is almost similar every year, though sometimes new sections are added or older ones eliminated. It ends in either Manali or Leh or even Srinagar, depending on the political situation. That year's route would take drivers over the 10,000 feet-high Jalori Pass, down to the tranquil Tirthan valley and then to the road running alongside the Beas into Manali. From Manali, we would go up to the Rohtang Pass and cross over into the barren district of Lahaul, from where we'd have to do the run from Gramphu to Chotta Dara and back, and then carry on towards Leh. The 480-kilometre road that runs from Manali to Leh traverses four high-altitude passes; it's traversable only from late May to late October. The rest of the year it remains snowed in.

The Raid-de-Himalaya runs during the second week of October and has always been blessed with good weather. I'd been on this road a number of times and have waxed eloquent about its almost divine beauty and the pleasure of motoring here. This is because, on all my previous forays, I've been blessed with a shining sun. My journeys here have always been leisurely ones, stopping at the various tea shacks set up by simple hill folk under huge parachute tents at Jispa, Darcha or Sarchu. And, every time, I've been taken aback by the stark and stunning landscape. It's a small wonder that people believe that it is here that the Gods reside. This particular year, however, we participants quickly realised, that yes, as stories tell us, this land is truly the abode of the Gods—it's just that sometimes the Devil comes visiting too, and nature is coerced into unleashing it full fury.

The weather was still wonderful as we powered our way up the Rohtang Pass; it seemed like it would be like just another drive in these mountains. I'd suggested taking one Dispirin and one Diamox to battle the high altitude, but Jack had unfortunately been overcautious and popped two Diamoxes. The result was a hyperactive bladder—he had to pee every twelve minutes. And the relief operation was a lengthy one because Jack was wearing about five layers of clothing. By the time he unbuttoned, unzipped, untied, pulled down, pulled out and let flow, many precious minutes had gone past. And this meant that I would have to drive even faster to make up for lost time on the narrow, unsealed roads.

'Look,' I said finally, 'the car's heated, so you can sit with your waterproof pants, track pants, jeans and long-johns at your knees. Just keep your underwear on and then when you want to go again, all you have to do is pull down your underwear and let loose. It will save us time.'

'That's a good idea,' he replied, nodding his head like a wobbly doll on the dashboard of a car.

We were now beyond Rohtang and driving on roads bordered with snow. The next time he wanted to go, Jack hopped out of the car and efficiently did his stuff. But when he was done, he lost his balance while trying to pull his underwear on again. The slippery ice and the restricted leg movement caused him to fall flat on his face on the ice. The ice was like oiled glass and, with most of his clothes around his knees, he couldn't get up his own. He lay there like a beached turtle, exposed rear end shining in the sun like a beacon, and bleating for help. By the time I gingerly made my way across, falling a few times myself, Jack had been lying with his face—and a lot of other things—in the ice for a considerable while.

Needless to say, he wasn't too enthusiastic about any of my suggestions after that.

Despite the delays, we didn't fare too badly on that first day. We were far down in the rankings, but at least the car was still intact despite being hammered on the atrocious roads that make up the final five kilometres of the approach to the Jalori Pass. The event ran quite smoothly the first three days. Jack was learning on the job. His grasp of mathematics and time, speed and distance was enviable, and within three days his spot-on calculations of what speed I should maintain (he even managed to factor in a quick stop for me at the Chotta Dara dhaba which serves the fantastic masala chai) and my somehow managing to maintain ridiculous speeds on those treacherous roads brought us up in the standings. We were amongst the top three when we rolled into the army camp at Pang.

This place, literally in the middle of nowhere, is strategically placed between two mountain passes. To the south of it lies the mighty Baralacha La which, at 16,040 feet, is the highest pass in Himachal Pradesh, and thirty kilometres to the north, standing at 17,582 feet, lies the imposing Tanglang La, the fourth highest motorable road in the world. This means that should both passes close due to snowfall, one could be stuck in Pang till one opened. When we'd crossed Baralacha La on the way to Pang, there was a lot of snow, but the road was clear thanks to the army that works round the clock to keep the roads open and motorable.

When we drove into Pang, the sun was shining in a clear blue sky, but don't let that lead you to believe that it was warm and toasty: even standing in bright sunlight, the temperature was still hovering at five degrees—below zero, that is.

Since we were being put up with the army, the accommodation was arranged in tin shack barracks with a single homemade heater stove for warmth. This of course was completely inadequate for when the sun set and the temperature went down to minus 20 degrees. Even as the sun started going down behind the tall mountains and began throwing long shadows, we all crowded the small areas still getting direct sunlight, much like amateur dancers hogging the spotlight in a competition. Even the Mess, which was covered and heated by two big stoves, was so cold that the tea put out in huge vacuum containers for the weary rallyists went from piping hot to stone cold in about four minutes.

All competitors had now transformed into moving masses of wool, because no matter how many layers of clothing you had on, the cold still crept in. Jack was wearing every stitch of clothing he'd brought and was yet shivering nonstop. And, while the cold was doing all it could to make us miserable on the outside, our heads were being hammered by the altitude, which at 15,190 feet is over four kilometres above sea level. For many of the rallyists, mountain sickness had started manifesting itself in the form of headaches, nausea and slight disorientation. The Indian-style loos were torture-tests of endurance because one had to endure the biting draft of the icy wind on your bare posterior to obtain bowel nirvana. All this besides the high level of driving skill required is what makes the Raid-de-Himalaya the gruelling event it is. The organisers warn potential participants that this is what they will have to go through and they better be prepared for it.

I like to think of the night halt at Pang as the big sieve, where the hardy are filtered from the weak. Mind you, it is not just physical fitness that helps a person survive these killer conditions. One may be in great physical shape, but up there, if the mental determination and 'I can handle this' spirit is lacking, one may well end up lying flat on one's back, crying for relief.

The places we'd stayed the two previous nights were five-star resorts compared to these flimsy shack shelters.

Already the fact that we were to spend two nights there had caused the faces of the more pampered competitors to fall. And mind you, while it was terribly cold, the weather was still calm. Not for very long though.

The next morning we had to do a run to Tanglang La and back—a round trip of sixty kilometres. Halfway through the climb up to the Pass, the snow started coming down. For most of us plains- and seaside-dwellers, snow was a novelty, and the gentle flakes were greeted with cheers and smiles of wonder. But soon the wispy snowfall became a full-fledged blizzard, much like a cuddly cub turns into a ferocious tiger. I remember stopping atop Tanglang La and stepping out of the heated interiors of my car to take a picture. The cold was a physical monster that wrapped its chilly arms around me and seemed to suck the last vestige of warmth out of me. The snowfall was unexpected so we had to maintain the stipulated average speed of 35kmph while coming down Tanglang La. You may scoff at this speed, which an Olympic sprinter achieves with ease, but coming down an iced-up road with steep inclines and mean hairpin bends is like walking a tightrope between two skyscrapers. One thousand-foot sheer drops were waiting to grab us should we veer off the road.

Because of the ice that had formed on the road, I had as much traction as a ball bearing on glass, a fact that

I didn't realise until when I was coming down an incline and had to brake to a sharp right turn. I dabbed the brake pedal and steered to the right, but nothing happened. The car continued to slide straight towards the edge. This is when I felt the slimy serpent of fear uncoil in my stomach. This is it! This is where I die! And so intense was the feeling of impending death that I actually saw my life scrolling across my mind like the stock ticker that runs at the bottom of a television screen on a business news channel. Frantic last-minute acceleration and a desperate grab at the handbrake saved us from going over the edge. Jack had gone as white as a funeral shroud and thenceforth sat with his seat belt unbuckled and door slightly ajar. If we were going to go over, he was going to jump, he declared. But from then on I drove down very cautiously. Jack didn't stop calculating the speed I needed to be driving at, and I managed to stick to it, even though we were sliding around corners heart-stoppingly close to the edges.

By the time we got back to Pang, there was a full-fledged blizzard blowing. The stark brown-gray mountains had turned white, the entire encampment had turned white—the whole world had turned white.

Even before any official notice was pasted in the Mess at camp, gloom seemed to spread like a premonition of the precarious position we were in. The weather gods had gone evil and were sending down snow at an alarming rate. We'd seen how Tanglang La was already packing up, and towards the south the mighty Baralacha La was also shutting it doors. This meant that if things didn't clear up soon, we'd be stuck in this open-air cold storage for days. And the very thought of that was enough to send a chill up our already severely frozen spines.

It continued to snow all through the day, letting off only towards evening. The next morning the organisers decided to make a break for it and we all lined up in a convoy for what would turn out to be the most harrowing drive of my life.

This beautiful road that I'd considered familiar territory showed me a side to it that made me understand how foolish it would be to ever take mountain roads for granted. The wind was howling across the mountains playing a sadistic tune to which our car—thanks to the snow and ice that coated the road like icing on a pineapple cake—danced the sideways salsa. It started snowing yet again as we began climbing the incline to the mighty Baralacha La. With the car fighting for grip on a narrow mountain ledge and the weather rapidly deteriorating, I once again got a terribly gloomy feeling that the curtains were starting to come down on my time as a human. There was one incline that I just couldn't seem to make because the car kept sliding down, the tyres spinning uselessly on the hard ice.But on my third attempt some celestial hand must have turned over the hourglass of my luck just as the grains were running out, and the little Alto we were in managed to find a semblance of traction on the ice crunched by my previous attempts, and just about managed to clear that icy crest. From then on it was all downhill, which was not particularly easy either. Here I had to fight gravity and had very little traction to combat its deadly pull down those mountain roads.

Past the towns of Patseo and Darcha and Jispa I drove in a merry slip and slide. The blizzard was going full force and visibility was down to a few feet. There was literally no room for error simply because there was no grip for correction. If I'd missed a corner, there would have been no hope of the car stopping before it went down over the edge. It was in these cold and hazardous conditions that we rolled into Keylong where news that the Rohtang Pass had shut was just filtering into town.

We checked into Hotel Chandra Bagha, Himachal Tourism's best effort north of Manali.

That little town of Keylong became our immensely pretty jail for four days as we waited for Rohtang to relent and let us through. We had food, drink, electricity and hot water, and even though we were stranded there, we considered ourselves enormously lucky.

We were the fifth car in the convoy, and the only

two-wheel drive car to clear that treacherous incline up Baralacha La. For the scores of cars behind us, it was just the beginning of an ordeal that has left them with bitter memories that come rushing back every time they feel the cold blast of air when they open refrigerators at home. They had to abandon their cars at Baralacha La, and were evacuated in army trucks and open-air Maruti Gypsys. Try to imagine travelling even ten kilometres in an open vehicle with temperatures touching minus 25 degrees Centigrade and snow descending relentlessly. It's quite easy to believe it was nothing short of a miracle that no souls floated across from one world to another on that cold and chilly October day.

Incidentally, Jack and I won that Raid-de-Himalaya, and it remains one of my proudest achievements. Every time I look at the magnificent trophy sitting in my study, I am transported back to those days when Jack and I battled extremely high odds, fought extreme weather and coaxed a small little Alto over high-altitude iced-out roads to win what has been arguably the toughest Raid-de-Himalaya to date.

The Animals

An Eye for More than the Tiger

NH 7 is one of India's arterial highways. It connects Varanasi to Kanyakumari, on the way linking Nagpur, Hyderabad, Bangalore and Madurai. If you drive 105 kilometres north of Nagpur on this highway, you'll come to Pench National Park, which straddles the Maharashtra and Madhya Pradesh border. Pench is where Akela, Bageera, Baloo and Mowgli dwelled—it is these jungles that Rudyard Kipling based his *Jungle Book* on.

It was 2008, and Taj Hotels had recently thrown open the doors of its magnificent Baghvan Resort there. Lovely secluded cottages with open-air bathrooms and cosy rooftop machaans that are candlelit and draped with translucent white curtains—it's a perfect place for couples. Sleeping in the machaan instead of inside the cottage is hugely exciting, as animal calls, including the bone-chilling call of a hungry tiger, wash over the machaan at night.

I'd driven up the NH 7 from Hyderabad to Nagpur, and Amanda had hopped onto the Mumbai-Nagpur evening flight. She breezed out of Nagpur airport's terminal building where I was waiting for her and hopped up to me like a monkey who's found an abandoned basket of bananas. Besides being happy to see me, she was ecstatic about making the flight.

Just two hours before she'd called me in tears. She had cut the journey to the airport too fine and a traffic jam en route meant she had arrived at the airport just twenty-five minutes before departure time, had rushed through security since she had already web-checked in and had carry-on luggage only. But the smartly-dressed young man at the boarding desk had shaken his head apologetically. 'Sorry Madam, I regret to inform you that boarding for this flight is now closed. Our ground staff will assist you in booking the morning flight to Nagpur.'

She'd called me and in between sobs apprised me about the entire drama at the departure gate. I told her to stand her ground and bawl unrelentingly in front of the departure desk, as loudly as she could.

Now Amanda is not exactly soft-spoken, and the normal volume of her voice is just a few decibels shy than that of an air raid warning siren. I'm quite certain that if you were to get a genealogist to trace her lineage, sitting on some branch of her family tree you'd find a town crier of the Mughal court. So obviously the sound of her sobbing must have caused quite a commotion in the departure holding area. The poor lad was now put on the backfoot; I bet his manual about 'handling situations' had not included anything like this. He stammered into his walkie-talkie, which he was holding in his left hand, and offered his neatly folded handkerchief to Amanda with the right.

'I . . . I . . . don't want your hanky. I . . . I . . . I want to get on the flight,' she cried, howling like a four-year-old whose sweet has been snatched away.

It worked. The airline's airport manager arrived at the gate and had her rushed across the tarmac in a crew car to the flight just as they were about to shut doors.

As soon as the Boeing 737 had reached cruising altitude, one of the flight attendants hurriedly prepared a hot cup of tea to soothe her, but when he got to her seat, she was fast asleep under a blanket, a content smile on her face.

She happily narrated all this to me as we drove from the airport to Baghvan. The drive took us about two hours and we were warmly welcomed by the staff just as it was getting to be dinner time.

Over the welcome drink (a Mahua Martini—mahua is the local liquor), Kunwar Singh, the resident naturalist, outlined the morning's plan for the safari into the park.

After that we sat in the machaan of our cottage sipping on hot chocolate laced with Irish whiskey. My drive from Hyderabad to Nagpur along the crowded highway, the cacophony of Nagpur and Amanda's incident at the airport all seemed to belong to a world very far away as we sat against the soft bolsters under a warm quilt listening to the bark of a deer, the hoot of a spotted owl and the occasional screech of a langur.

The next morning was safari time and we were awoken by a gentle knocking on the door. It was our butler who had arrived at the dot of 5.45 a.m. bearing a tray of cookies and tea in a fine china teapot and matching cups. It was strong and stiff wake-up tea.

It's a cardinal rule of safaris that the earlier you get up, the bigger your chance of seeing wildlife. Amanda, like Garfield, doesn't do mornings. So I had to sleepwalk her to the bathroom, hand her the toothpaste and toothbrush and get her going. Then I had to regularly check in on her in case she'd dozed off inside the bathroom. When we finally emerged from our suite at about 6.45 a.m., Kunwar Singh was waiting for us, sharply dressed in khakis and a wide-brimmed hat. He was to be our man about the jungle. Both of us had our 'Where is the tiger? Show me a tiger!' expression on our faces and Kunwar Singh told us that the elephants and their mahouts were out in the jungle looking for tiger tracks. They would almost certainly come across a few, which could lead them to where the tiger had settled down for the morning.

'But till then there is the rest of the jungle to enjoy.' So saying he switched off the car engine and silence descended on us. But as I listened, I realised that the jungle was far from silent. On the periphery of my hearing I heard, like the whistle of a train emerging from a faraway tunnel, the cry of an eagle and looked up to see a crested hawk eagle circling the sky above in a graceful glide. It had probably spotted some prey and was now in observation mode. It didn't need to flap its wings because, as the sun grew stronger, hot air thermals rose from the ground and the eagle was buoyant on one of these. Closer to us, a Red-Wattled Lapwing was persistently calling out its characteristic 'did-you-do-it' call.

We drove around a little, spotting ducks sitting symmetrically on a log in a stream, some jackals running about with their tongues hanging out, and even a fat, lazy python.

We stopped at a little clearing where the sun was visible above the tree tops. Kunwar Singh turned to an olive green hamper and pulled out a shiny thermos from it. Next emerged a plastic box filled with freshly-baked muffins. Kunwar Singh neatly spread out a tablecloth on a large, flat rock and arranged plates and napkins. He then unfolded little camp stools and arranged them around the rock, and our mid-morning picnic was set and ready to be enjoyed. We were just enjoying the chocolate chip muffins and the sweet, hot and gingery tea (to chase the chill away), served in steel safari mugs complete with twine wrapped around the handles to act as insulation from the heat, when suddenly from his high-rise in the jungle, a langur gave a short bark-like cough, much like a teenager after taking his first hesitant drag of a cigarette. Kunwar Singh froze with his mug halfway to his lips and whispered what we'd been waiting to hear all morning, 'Tiger.'

The simian had spotted the striped cat and was now calling out regularly, warning jungle folk that the predator was on the move. Kunwar Singh hurriedly bundled up tablecloth, thermos, mugs and Tupperware, shoved it unceremoniously into the hamper and we started off once again. By now other monkeys had taken up the call and Kunwar Singh followed the direction of these. We came to a stop on a narrow jungle track and the car was switched off again.

'If this is the tiger I think it is, he will almost certainly cross the path from here. I've often seen his pug marks. He prefers this route to the waterhole.'

He was right: in a few minutes, a magnificent male tiger stepped out of the jungle and paused in the middle of the track. But instead of crossing to the other side, he started walking on the track. We followed him for a full fifteen minutes. At one point, when we tried to reduce the distance between him and the car, he stopped, turned around and gave out an angry roar. It was a warning, telling us in no uncertain terms to keep a respectful distance.

Post the tiger sighting, we let Kunwar Singh show us around the rest of the jungle. Pench has a bounty of birds and our naturalist had them down pat. He pointed out Indian Rollers, Drongos and even the elusive Paradise Flycatcher. At a gnarled, old tree which had a hollow at the juncture where its trunk branched out into a lopsided Y, he showed us a little owl that was peeking out, looking at us with its big round eyes. He explained that the eyes, besides making the nocturnal bird look hauntingly beautiful, also collect ambient light to help the owl see better in the dark.

Along with spotting birds, stories kept rolling out about animal habits, trees and how the flower of the mahua or Butter tree is used to make the smooth local liquor that has an aftershock like the angry kick of a very stubborn mule.

Almost every national park has a sign which more or less conveys that you shouldn't just be on the watch-out for a tiger but enjoy the entire jungle and its inhabitants so that you aren't disappointed. It was on this visit to Pench that the jungle, which I used to consider a home and larder for tigers, my sole purpose for visiting a national park, suddenly became much more than just about seeing the big cat. Kunwar Singh, through his stories and sightings, showed us on that morning safari in Pench that there was so much to see if you put your mind off the cat and devoted your eyes and ears to the surroundings.

The Devious Donkeys of Dasada

These wild asses were making an ass out of me. And what was annoying me even more was that it seemed to me that as they stood there together, looking like a handsome group of tawny ponies and swishing their tails and flicking their long ears—which gave away the fact that they were donkeys—it was as if they were nonchalantly discussing what a gullible idiot I was.

Woking on a story about a driving holiday to the Rann of Kutch, I wanted to get a perfect shot of a herd of the Asiatic wild ass running on the Little Rann of Kutch, which is believed to be their last remaining habitat.

Up until now, everything had gone like clockwork. A friend of mine, nicknamed Pal, and I had driven a Toyota Innova from Mumbai to Zainabad, Gujarat in a long slog on NH 8 and National Expressway 1. We'd done the 650-odd kilometres in about ten hours. (The NE 1, or the Mahatma Gandhi Expressway, which runs from Baroda to Ahmedabad, must be one of India's smoothest roads: it is ultra modern with well-designed entry and exit ramps and lucid and standard signage.) We'd spent the night at the Rann Riders at Zainabad. This is a place that tries to give its guests an authentic yet comfortable rural Gujarat experience. So while the walls of the cottages are caked cow dung, air-conditioners keep temperatures down when needed.

The next morning, with a local lad called Zubair acting as guide and with Pal at the wheel, we had set off towards Dasada, a village about ten kilometres from Zainabad on the periphery of the huge salt pans that make up the Little Rann of Kutch. The Little Rann of Kutch is a vast, flat and almost featureless expanse. Once you're in it, the only fixed orientation you have is the position of the sun in the sky with reference to the time of day. Zubair was there to show us the way in and out and also to guide us past treacherous bogs that the Rann is peppered with. Some of them can be easily spotted, and an alert eye can prevent you from going into them. The dangerous ones are those that lie beneath a thin layer of sturdy-looking silt or topsoil. Drive on this and you'll find your car bogged in salt and mud that has the consistency of oatmeal porridge.

With Zubair's guidance we made our way into the Rann, crossing a railway track at a makeshift level-crossing that the locals used. Our plan had seemed simple: find a herd of asses, do some sort of game drive to herd them such that the sun was in their faces, get a few cracking shots with this warm morning light and get out of the Rann.

It was a plan that should have worked except that these asses were turning out to be Rommel reincarnates. They would neatly break into two groups and veer left and right in such synchronised manoeuvres that even Montgomery would have saluted the precision of it all. I was hanging out of the car window, fancy camera in hand, and had not yet taken a single passable shot. Pal was trying to align the car with the sun as well as the asses and was basically going round and round in rapid circles because those damn animals kept shifting the axis of the chase. Zubair, unaccustomed to transportation that moved so fast and turned so rapidly within such a small radius, was fighting to keep his morning tea within the confines of his stomach and was going green in the process.

Finally we stopped to take stock of the situation, and Zubair tumbled out of the car, happy to be on firm ground. The asses, finally stationary, had also grouped together and now seemed to be discussing what a refreshing exercise it had been.

Irritated with the sight of the herd standing smugly in the distance, I told my crew that we'd give it another go. This time the strategy I outlined was to use the car's superior speed and just pull alongside one bunch of the asses and get some pictures. We started off; so did the donkeys, and the chase was on. Strangely, this time as we drew closer, the asses just herded together tighter and continued to run hard. This seemed to be working better than I expected, I commented, looking back at Zubair. Our guide's battle with the tea in the belly was now being fought in his gullet and he had his hand firmly clamped over his mouth to avoid any mishap.

Now we were close enough to the herd for me to hear the dull drumming of their hoofs on the baked surface of the salt pans. I was quite amazed at the speeds they were capable of. Pal yelled that the car was doing almost 70kmph and we were just about keeping up with the herd.

I finally got close enough to start shooting and furiously started tripping the camera's shutter. But ten seconds later the herd executed a scathing left turn— each and every one of the asses turned so hard that some of them went down on their haunches. The kind of sharp turn you see a zebra make on Nat Geo when it is trying to escape from a lioness. I was shocked at the collective adroitness of the asses, as was Pal. Stunned, we looked at each other, wondering what the hell had just happened.

The car was still going straight ahead at 70kmph when Zubair yelled out a sudden warning, muffled by his hand over his mouth. His other hand was pointing urgently ahead, eyes wide with horror. Even though Pal hit the brakes instantly, it was too late. The asses had swerved hard to avoid a bog, and we'd driven straight into it. It may sound silly, but I think that was the herd's game plan to get us off their collective tails once and for all. They really did seem as if they had led us in the direction of the bog and then swerved hard to avoid it at the very last moment.

Fortunately, Zubair's warning had saved us from total disaster: we'd skidded to a stop on the fringe of the bog rather than driven right into its soft centre, but the car was still stuck fast. Any attempt to back it out only resulted in the wheels spinning on the spot and the car sinking further into the soft slush. Zubair and I kicked off our shoes, rolled up our trousers and walked into the clayey grime to push the car out while Pal stayed at the wheel, but it was soon clear that the two of us weren't manpower enough. We needed help. Fortunately, though we were in the middle of the flat Rann, featureless till the horizon in every direction, we were in cellular range. Zubair whipped out his phone and sent an SOS to his friends Sailesh, Kamlesh and Nilesh.

Now, calling them and having them arrive were two different things, not because the trio lacked enthusiasm or a desire to help, but the mad chase had left us bereft of any sense of direction. I had to climb onto the roof of the car and pan the horizon with field glasses for the railway line that was our only landmark. Half an hour after our location was communicated, Zubair's pals arrived on a battered old Rajdoot. Even with the five of us pushing, the car refused to budge. I finally had to dig out the mud and slush from around the wheels; only then did we manage to get it unstuck. On the way back, the grime dried around my hands and forearms like a plaster cast. Even the tyres were packed with the mud that was rapidly drying around them. So heavy was the weight of this mud that the steering, even with the power-assist, felt dull and cumbersome.

We took a different route out of the Rann, on the way meeting a group of nomads camped with their livestock. The men were dressed in magnificent white turbans and hobnailed sandals of camel leather, and the womenfolk were wearing backless cholis and thick white bangles that covered almost the entire length of their arms. The head of the group invited us to a simple meal of fat bajra rotis and garlic chutney that was spicy and sharp, accompanied with milky tea made with thick, sweet and creamy camel milk, served in earthen cups. They were in the middle of preparing their evening meal using the khad method, the unique cooking process used by nomadic tribes in the Northwest frontier, which involves digging a pit, burying the meat and allowing it to cook with the heat of the sand.

I was quite happy to exit the Rann and be back on hard tarmac and a considerable distance from those devious donkeys. At the first little village we stopped at the communal hand pump and I pretty much had a bath under it to remove the stubborn soil from my hands and feet. I think the entire village must have turned up to watch.

Not quite successful as I had hoped to be at getting my wild ass shots, I decided to try my photography skills on a more cooperative subject—the Sun temple at Modhera that has been standing in the same place since 1027 AD when it was built by King Bhimdev I.

Modhera is about fifty kilometres from Dasada, and even though it was well into the day when we got there, apart from a few locals lounging about, we pretty much had the place to ourselves. The temple is truly a beautiful piece of Indian architecture. Its flowing lines and symmetry would make anyone who looks at it salute those ancient architects who designed it. It is about two hundred years older than the Sun temple at Konark, but I felt it had stood the test of time more handsomely. The temple is adorned with figures. Like the sculptors at Khajuraho, these stonemasons also preferred their women voluptuous and their mallets and chisels have given form to lovely apsaras and dancing girls all over the temple walls.

While today tourists come with cameras and pilgrims come with garlands and flowers, Zubair told me that the most unwelcome visitor here was Alauddin Khilji who, after his conquest of Gujarat at the end of the thirteenth century, let loose sledgehammer-wielding legions on the temple in an attempt to destroy it. It is an eternal snub on the emperor that, even today, almost one thousand years on, the temple, the curvaceous apsaras and the sexual poses carved on the walls continue to wow those who come to visit.

Photographing the temple and its stunningly artistic Surya Kund (stepwell) made up for the futile wild ass chase earlier in the day.

Jolly Jhunjhunwalla and the Great Bus Chase

*B*etween Delhi and Panipat, on old Sher Shah Suri's Grand Trunk Road, is a place called Murthal which is 25 kilometres or so past the Delhi–Haryana border. There's an array of restaurants here, typical highway eateries, lining the left side of the road. I have often stopped here while driving from Delhi to the Himalayas. A 4.45 a.m. start from Delhi usually gets me there by 6 a.m., ready for a cup of morning tea.

A few years back I was driving to Amritsar where I

was planning to meet my parents and take them for a road trip to Kashmir and Ladakh. Since we would be spending several days in the car from Amritsar onwards, they'd decided to take the comfortable Shatabdi Express from Delhi to Amritsar.

Traffic had been minimal after Murthal, and the fuel-injected Maruti Esteem that I was driving was quite the highway star. I was enjoying my new iPod, the surprising paucity of traffic and the enthusiasm of the car when, at Gharunda, just before Karnal, I encountered a minor traffic snarl. Gharunda is another place where there is a battery of restaurants, and tourist buses and taxis often stop here. I was waiting for passengers to climb into the bus ahead, trying to judge whether I could turn the wheels a full right and pull out from behind it, when suddenly there was a frantic rapping of knuckles on the car's front left window. Startled, I turned to see a hairy visage, eyes bulging, looking in at me. While one hand was frantically knocking on the window, I could see that the other was clutching half a sandwich. The other half of the sandwich was stuffed in the mouth that was now asking me to roll down the window.

I did so and the man shoved his face in and said, 'Helloji, my name is Jolly Jhunjhunwalla. Please, please, please, bus gone, chase chase.' By the time these words were spoken, most of the sandwich had been sprayed onto my front passenger seat.

I asked the man to calm down a bit, take a few deep breaths and for god's sake swallow that sandwich and then continue talking.

In short, his tale of woe was that he was on a bus to Chandigarh which had stopped there to give its passengers a fifteen-minute breakfast break. Jolly had gone ahead and ordered a three-course breakfast and the first course had arrived six minutes later. He was halfway through it when the driver had fired up the bus after just ten minutes were up; tooted the horn fifteen seconds later to warn passengers; and driven off thirty seconds after that. Another bus had immediately pulled into the parking spot left vacant by the departing bus. Jolly, blissfully unaware about what had just happened, had stepped out from the restaurant to pop into the bus and get his daily dose of blood pressure medicine. He stepped into the bus and was surprised to find a monkey-cap-clad Bengali sitting on his seat. His bags in the overhead luggage shelves too seemed to have changed colour and size. He quickly realised what had happened, and roundly cursed the driver of his bus. Now, his bulging eyes told me, he needed his high blood pressure pills more than ever.

'Please I need your help to catch up with the bus,' he earnestly requested. I quite understood the jam Jolly was in. And, I had a quick car that was light on its wheels because I was hardly carrying any luggage. I was sure I could catch up with the bus soon.

'Okay get in, let's go and catch your bus,' I told him cheerily, excited at the prospect of a chase.

'One minute please,' he replied and trotted back into the restaurant. He emerged with two buxom ladies flanking him, one of them still with a glass of tea in her hand.

'My wife and sister-in-law,' he explained with a smile. I was taken aback. All this time I had assumed that Jolly was travelling alone. And then I realised that he hadn't even told them what had happened. As he proceeded to do so, the sister-in-law almost fainted. All her jewellery was in her bag, she said, and her bag was on the bus that was now speeding towards Ambala without them on board. The wife began screaming at Jolly about being so greedy and careless. 'I told you, we should have packed the sandwiches and eaten them on the bus. What was the need to order parathas? All your life you've eaten parathas for breakfast! What difference would it have made if you did not have them today?'

I felt very sorry for poor Jolly. I got out and helped him herd the two women—one swooning and the other screeching—into the back seat of the car and told him to pop in the remainder of the sandwich, swallow it completely and then get into the front passenger seat.

The Esteem was no longer as swift as it had felt thanks to the dead weight stacked on the rear seat. The swooning sister-in-law had recovered and was now bawling away. Jolly's wife was asking him to contact one of their relatives who happened to know the secretary of the road transport minister. I still haven't figured out how that might have helped.

Jolly was hanging out of the window, trying to get a look at the drivers of the buses we were rapidly overtaking, although I did point out that his bus would have already covered a lot of distance and there was no chance that we'd catch up with it so soon.

When I asked him if he remembered the registration number, he sorrowfully shook his head. But the sister-in-law stopped her steady drone for a moment, reached into her handbag and pulled out the booking slip that the travel agent had given them. On it was the registration number of the bus.

We'd already wasted a lot of time at Gharunda and were now mired in rush-hour traffic while driving past Karnal. Fortunately, after this the road opened up a bit and traffic cleared. I gave the Esteem a loose reign and we were soon doing 120kmph and overtaking other traffic on the road. At times I had to apply the brakes hard, swing in and swing out rapidly to maintain our average speed. All cacophony from the rear seat stopped completely. I glanced into the rear view mirror and saw Jolly's wife and sister-in-law holding on to each other, faces white with fear. Jolly, on the other hand, seemed to be enjoying this spirited driving, and I suspected that at some level he was taking sadistic satisfaction from the women's terror.

I'd been giving chase for over an hour and 85 kilometres, and was seriously starting to consider the possibility that I'd overtaken the bus without realising it. If this was the case, I'd have to stop and wait, but then if it wasn't, I'd only widen the gap between us and the bus. I was pondering this dilemma when Jolly gave a whoop of joy and pointed ahead. Their bus was seventy-five meters ahead. I flashed my lights and tooted my horn as I drew up alongside the bus, trying to indicate to the driver that he should pull up and stop by the side of the road. That dolt took my audio-visual display of urgency as a challenge and cut right across my nose, upped his speed and started pulling away. This manoeuvre of his sent Jolly's blood pressure sky-rocketing and once again his eyes bulged out a disturbing distance from their sockets. I took up the gauntlet thrown down by the bus driver and chased after him.

We were getting close to Shahpur and traffic was quite heavy. I had to dodge cars and trucks, swinging left and right to keep up with the bus. In the rear seat the women were enveloped in each other's fleshy arms, their faces a picture of petrified piety as they looked skywards. I drew up alongside the bus again till Jolly's window was alongside the bus driver.

'Stop the bus at once,' he yelled, his face an alarmingly bright red.

The bus driver sniggered at him and said, 'This bus will only stop in Ambala now, catch me if you can.'

I was just thinking that I'd have to pull a Bollywood-like manoeuvre and force him off the road when we came to a red light. Traffic had stopped and so the bus driver had to also stand on the brakes and come to a halt. To be honest, it was quite an anti-climactic end to the chase.

Jolly was out of the car in a flash. I tried to tell him to take it easy, but he was in a rage beyond reason. He yanked open the bus driver's door and pulled the man out of the cabin like a sack of potatoes and gave him two tight slaps as a preamble to the argument.

The two women were still in the car, stiff with open-mouthed terror. Assuming they'd need time to recover, I rushed to the bus driver's aid, who Jolly had now propped against the front tyre and was steadily beating to pulp. The other passengers of the bus had also rushed out and were now trying to pull Jolly off the driver who was cowering in fright. All his bravado had disappeared and he collapsed in a heap by the tyre of the bus.

'Arrey puttar if you beat him up, who will drive the bus to Chandigarh,' one passenger yelled, trying to make Jolly see reason.

That worked and Jolly bent over the driver, gave him two more tight slaps to bring him out of his stupor and promised more of the same if he didn't come to his senses at once. The driver stood straight immediately. He'd felt enough of Jolly's fat fist against his face; he was ready to drive till China if need be to avoid further application of the same. But he was still shaking like a leaf. One of the passengers, a kind old lady, pulled out a shiny thermos and poured the driver some tea, which he sipped on to steady his nerves.

He was halfway through the tea when Jolly's wife and sister-in-law, now fully recovered, arrived on the scene. Both of them also wanted to add two-three slaps to the kitty of pasting that the driver had accumulated, causing the poor chap to tremble so violently that the remainder of the tea spilled over the sides of his cup. But, once again, the crowd restrained them.

All three of them then got onto the bus, checked that their luggage was safe and came back down to thank me.

Finally with all passengers onboard this time, the bus started off towards Chandigarh.

I've driven that road plenty of times after that, and every time I drive past the signal where we finally got the bus to stop, I can't help thinking of Jolly Jhunjhunwalla and the great bus chase.

'May We Please Kindly Burn Your Car?'

They take their strikes very seriously in Kerala. If a bandh or strike has been declared, then it is very rare that you'll find people ignoring it. This means life comes to a complete standstill. You can't go to work nor can you venture out on the roads.

I was at the Periyar National Park in Kumily, Kerala. It was March 2002. I had spent three eventful days there, floating down the river on a boat, walking in the jungle with a ranger and even spending a night camping near the forest. Now I was ready to continue my trip and my next destination was Munnar, which is about 115 kilometres from Kumily.

As it turned out, the day I was to leave was declared a bandh in protest against the tragic Godhra train burning incident that had taken place the previous month. The hotel staff earnestly advised me not to risk driving to Munnar before 6 p.m., at which time the bandh would end. The 115 kilometres would take me about two-and-a-half hours and I'd be in Munnar by 8.30 p.m., they said.

This sounded like a safe enough plan, and at the dot of 6 p.m., I started off in the little silver Maruti Zen that I'd picked up from a dealer in Cochin. I was to return it there when I finished my assignment in Kerala.

I was really enjoying the drive: the roads were empty and I was able to keep the speedometer needle hovering at 90kmph. It looked like I would make Munnar in less than two hours.

The villages I zipped through were practically deserted. The few people I saw all pointed at my car with a look of surprise on their faces. I thought it a little surprising, but didn't dwell on it much.

The non-existence of vehicles to overtake or joust with made the drive a little monotonous, and I soon started looking for a place to stop for a hot cup of tea. I especially wanted tea, since I had been on coffee ever since I'd arrived in Kerala. Filter coffee, flamboyantly poured from one shiny steel cup to another to work up a golden brown froth, is a respected beverage in this state. Since I was driving towards Munnar, which is surrounded by tea estates, I figured that my chances of getting a good cup of tea would be quite high. But all the shops in the villages and towns I drove through had their shutters down.

I had just crossed Nedumkandam when I came across a small settlement. There were just about seven-eight houses—too small to even call it a village. But there were some people gathered around the porch of one of the houses, and I could see that they were sipping from shiny steel cups.

I braked to a halt, got out of the car, locked it and walked up to them, and asked them where I could also get a cup of tea. Their faces reflected a terrified surprise and most of them rapidly walked away till there was just one elderly gentleman left standing with me. This gent was dressed in a spotless white shirt and lungi and he pointed to a tea shop that also served as a PCO tucked between two houses. I thanked him and walked to it.

The moment the master brewer of the shop saw me arrive, he switched off his stove and slammed the door shut, muttering 'Ille, ille', and shaking his head and both his hands. I tried to reason with him that I just wanted one cup of tea, but he kept shaking his head.

Suddenly his furiously shaking head froze and his eyes went wide in horror. He was staring at something behind me with such terror that I swung around immediately and recoiled in shock. There were five men standing around my parked car. They were dressed in black kurtas and lungis and their foreheads were smeared with three horizontal stripes of ash and a solitary vertical stripe of bright red vermillion. But what was most disturbing was that these fancy-dress annas were holding flaming torches in their hands.

By now the master brewer of the tea shop was trying to nonchalantly tend to the folds of his lungi, conveying that he had nothing to do with me.

I walked back to my car, trying to be casual about it. I wanted to get in and drive away as fast I could since this scene was taking on a very sinister hue. One of the lungi-clad men deftly stepped in front of the driver's door, making his intention very clear—I wasn't going to be driving anywhere.

He yelled out to me in Malayalam, which unfortunately I don't understand. Another joined in, and from the tone of their voices I knew that they weren't asking me to their houses for a cup of tea.

'Sorry, I don't understand,' I replied, trying to appear very blasé about the whole situation, and making a steadfast attempt to ignore the burning torches which were crackling away merrily around me.

The gentleman in white, who had directed me to the tea store, walked up to me and said, 'I know English. Could I be acting as your translator to be able to tell you what these fine gentlemen are trying to communicate with yourself?' The man was obviously very proud of his knowledge of the language and was trying to crowd in as many words as he could in a sentence to impress me with his vast vocabulary.

I replied that I would be very grateful if he would do so.

A few sentences of rapid Malayalam were exchanged between the group of black lungis and my representative in the white. The man blocking my door seemed to be the leader of the black lungis; he was talking sternly to white lungi, emphasising his sentences by pointing his index fingers at me and then my car.

My interpreter came up to me with an apologetic expression and said, 'I am sorry but you have offended these people by driving on the road today when it is a bandh day. So they are now wanting to be kindly burning your car.'

I reeled back in shock, and white lungi hurriedly added by way of consolation, 'But don't worry, I have convinced them to burn it without locking you inside it. That is good news no?' he declared, as if he'd won a great diplomatic victory for me.

By now one of the black lungis had obtained a plastic

jerry can and was about to start splashing petrol over my little Zen.

'Can't you bargain with them?' I asked white lungi urgently. 'Tell them that I'll give them the spare tyre to burn. I'll also add some of my socks and underwear for effect and even take a few pictures of the whole thing and then get it published in a newspaper so that these budding arsonists can have their moment of fame. It will make a nice little bonfire. Why burn the whole car?'

White lungi meticulously unfolded and refolded his lungi, no doubt buying time to translate all this into Malayalam and put it across as delicately as possible. He walked to the black lungis with all the gravity of a messenger on whose diplomatic skills depended world peace.

My proposal was rejected and by the alacrity with which white lungi came running back, I think they had threatened to burn him with the car too if he came up with any more insulting suggestions like giving them old underwear to burn.

I was at my wits' end and was trying to figure out how to get my camera out of the car before they torched it, when—like the cavalry arriving to the rescue of a besieged homestead—a highway patrol jeep arrived, its siren blazing.

Seeing the jeep, the black lungi with the jerry can immediately tried to get it open and splash some petrol over the car so that they could set it alight before the police intervened. I ran to him and kicked the can out of his hand just as the cops emerged from the jeep shouting. They made the black lungis douse their torches and herded them into the jeep. The chief inspector asked me where I was headed. When I told him Munnar was my destination, he said, 'Drive straight there, don't stop anywhere or for anybody.'

Before he left I thanked him for arriving at the nick of time. He told me that they were based in Nedumkandam and one of the locals had received a telephone call about what was happening and informed them about the same. They had rushed here as soon as they could.

After they had driven away, I went back to the tea shop. I really needed that cup of tea now. The master brewer was smiling at me now. He already had a cup of strong tea ready for me and my friend in the white lungi. As I sipped on it, he nonchalantly drummed his fingers on his telephone, smiling all the time.

Realisation hit me like a lightning bolt. It was he who had made that critical telephone call!

Acknowledgements

*H*ot Tea across India is a result of two of my hobbies, travel and writing, and I'd like to acknowledge those who helped me on my journeys and encouraged me to write.

My parents for my superb genes, a very good education and for inculcating the wonder of wandering, thanks to a childhood filled with eventful driving holidays in an old 1947 DeSoto and 1954 Dodge.

Ujjwal Mehta, my elder cousin, who filled my teenage years with plenty of books and who introduced me to the joy of long distance motorcycling.

ACKNOWLEDGEMENTS

Hormazd Sorabjee, editor of *Autocar India*, for giving me a job that had me going on a driving holiday to exotic locations in India every month for eight years! And for helping me hone my photography skills. Road trips and photoshoots with Hormazd are happy highlights of my years with *Autocar India*.

Maneck Davar of Spenta Multimedia for his continual encouragement and support right from when I was struggling to gain a foothold in travel writing.

Chetan Popat and Shapur Kotwal, my two closest friends, who have always been willing party to the plan, no matter how audacious the adventure.

Alpana Lath Sawai, former editor of *Sunday Mid-Day* who always enthusiastically accepted and encouraged my crazy and adventure-filled travelogues.

Prakash Thakur, my very dear friend in Thanedar. No matter what time of day or month of year I've called, Thakur Saab has always had hot and sweet masala chai, a tasty meal and a warm, cosy bed ready for me at Banjara Retreat at a moment's notice.

John Fernandes, ostensibly *Autocar India*'s editorial assistant but in reality 'the fixer'. Often while on the road I've needed air tickets or accommodation booked or money wired at a moment's notice; one call to John and it's been sorted.

G.K. Singh of *Autocar India*'s Delhi office for his invaluable help on my road trips starting from Delhi.

ACKNOWLEDGEMENTS

Capt Ajay Sud and Rajesh Ojha of Banjara Camps and Retreats—it is thanks to them that I feel at home in the Kinnaur and Spiti districts of Himachal Pradesh.

Vaibhav Kala of Aquaterra Adventures, which has rafting camps on the Ganga and the Tons. Both have often been lovely places to unwind after days of driving in the Himalayas.

My friends Navaz and Karandip Sandhu in Chandigarh—their home has often been a comfortable relief after days of roughing it out in the Himalayas.

My secondary school English teacher Mrs Nina Peters (nee Ashtamkar) who taught me how to wield the English language as a tool to give free reign to humour and imagination.

My editor, Deepthi Talwar, for giving my manuscript wonderful form and flow.

And, most of all, my sister Toranj, who is both my most brutal critic and my biggest fan.